UNDERSTANDING MILITARY CULTURE

Understanding Military Culture

A Canadian Perspective

ALLAN D. ENGLISH

McGill-Queen's University Press
Montreal & Kingston • London • Ithaca

ISBN 0-7735-2664-1 (cloth)
ISBN 0-7735-2715-X (paper)

Legal deposit first quarter 2004
Bibliothèque nationale du Québec

Printed in Canada on acid-free paper that is 100% ancient forest free (100% post-consumer recycled), processed chlorine free.

This book has been published with the help of a grant from the Canadian Forces Leadership Institute.

McGill-Queen's University Press acknowledges the support of the Canada Council for the Arts for our publishing program. We also acknowledge the financial support of the Government of Canada through the Book Publishing Industry Development Program (BPIDP) for our publishing activities.

This study was prepared for the Canadian Department of National Defence but the views expressed in it are solely those of the author. They do not necessarily reflect the policy or the opinion of any agency, including the Government of Canada and the Canadian Department of National Defence.

National Library of Canada Cataloguing in Publication

English, Allan D. (Allan Douglas), 1949–
Understanding military culture: a Canadian perspective / Allan D. English

Includes bibliographical references and index.
ISBN 0-7735-2664-1 (bnd)
ISBN 0-7735-2715-X (pbk)

1. Sociology, Military – Canada. 2. Sociology, Military – United States. I. Title.

UA600.E54 2004 306.2′7′0971 C2003-905088-2

This book was typeset by Dynagram Inc. in 10.5/13 Palatino.

This book is dedicated to my wife, Gina Gushue,

and my children, Meredith and Kyle English,

whose love and support

made this book possible.

Table of Contents

Foreword

REAR ADMIRAL DAVID MORSE
COMMANDER, CANADIAN DEFENCE ACADEMY

The Canadian Defence Academy (CDA) was created in 2002 to champion, govern, and manage professional development reform initiatives in the Canadian Forces (CF). The CDA will also be a body to institutionalize and maintain the momentum behind these reforms, which contribute to the CF's strategic objectives for professional development. Key among these objectives are fostering intellectual development and critical thinking within Canada's military and the transformation of the CF into a learning organization. The Chief of the Defence Staff, General R.R. Henault, put it this way: "Professional development is at the heart of the Profession of Arms. The CDA will play a vital role in the reform and transformation of our professional standards and competencies."

The publication of this book is one of a number of initiatives taken by the CDA to stimulate debate about the profession of arms in Canada. Readers are invited to join the debate and make their own contribution to military professionalism in this country.

Foreword

CAPT (N) A.C. OKROS
DIRECTOR, CANADIAN FORCES LEADERSHIP INSTITUTE

This is one in a series of publications sponsored by the Canadian Forces Leadership Institute (CFLI). The purpose of these publications is to disseminate ideas about leadership not only to members of the Department of National Defence but also to a wider audience of those who have an interest in military leadership.

This study is particularly timely because of the ongoing debate about how military culture in this country is related to the military cultures of our allies and how differing military cultures impact upon multinational operations. There is also a vigorous debate in some parts of the Canadian Forces over the nature of military culture in this country and how this affects the Canadian military's roles as war fighters, peacekeepers, and as part of Canadian society. With this book, the CFLI makes a contribution to this debate. Readers are encouraged to contact the Institute or the author if they have any questions or would like to pursue the issues examined in this study in more depth.

Preface

This study originated as a request from Lieutenant-General Romeo Dallaire to investigate the "Americanization" of the Canadian officer corps as part of his research program as Special Advisor to the Chief of Defence Staff on Officer Professional Development. Some preliminary findings were published as "The Americanization of the Canadian Officer Corps: Myth and Reality?" in Bernd Horn's *Contemporary Issues in Officership: A Canadian Perspective*. The analysis of the phenomenon of military culture found in this book came about as a result of a request by Dr Ross Pigeau, head of the Command Group at Defence Research and Development Canada (DRDC) – Toronto, to investigate these issues in a more detailed way in a Canadian context.

The author would like to thank Lieutenant-General Dallaire, Lieutenant-Colonel Horn, Dr Pigeau, and Carol McCann, also of DRDC – Toronto, for their encouragement in the writing of this study. The author is also grateful to the Canadian Forces Leadership Institute, especially its director, Capt (N) Alan Okros, for its support in publishing this study.

Abbreviations

AMSC	Advanced Military Studies Course
CBC	Canadian Broadcasting Corporation
CDA	Canadian Defence Academy
CDS	Chief of the Defence Staff
CF	Canadian Forces
CFLI	Canadian Forces Leadership Institute
CGSC	Command and General Staff College
CINC	Commander-in-Chief
CSIS	Center for Strategic and International Studies
DND	Department of National Defence
DRDC	Defence Research and Development Canada
IDF	Israeli Defence Forces
MND	Minister of National Defence
MRG	Management Review Group
MWO	Master Warrant Officer
NATO	North Atlantic Treaty Organization
NCM	non-commissioned member
NCO	non-commissioned officer
NDA	National Defence Act
NDHQ	National Defence Headquarters
NGO	non-governmental organization
NORAD	North American Aerospace Defence Command
OOTW	operations other than war
RAF	Royal Air Force
RCAF	Royal Canadian Air Force
RCF	Royal Flying Corps
RCN	Royal Canadian Navy

RMA	Revolution in Military Affairs
RMC	Royal Military College of Canada
RN	Royal Navy
UN	United Nations
UNEF	United Nations Emergency Force
USMC	United States Marine Corps
USN	United States Navy

UNDERSTANDING MILITARY CULTURE

1

Introduction

Change has been a constant companion of Canada's armed forces during the last half of the twentieth century. Demobilization after the Second World War was followed by a period of Cold War expansion and rearmament in the 1950s and early 1960s. The experience of integration and unification – merging the three services (the Royal Canadian Navy, the Royal Canadian Air Force, and the Canadian Army) into one legal entity in the late 1960s and the 1970s – resulted in significant changes to the structure of the Canadian Forces (CF). "Disintegration" (organizational and uniform changes that marked the return of the three services in appearance if not in name) and substantial downsizing in the 1980s and 1990s threw the CF into further disarray. Since the Second World War, an underlying theme in discussions of this change has been the degree to which the CF have become "Americanized" and what effects this might have on them. One of the few published analyses to deal directly with this issue offers a pessimistic assessment of the chances for the survival of a unique identity for Canada's armed forces. Granatstein noted that ideological similarities and geography make it very likely that Canada's defence policies will constantly move "in tandem" with American policies, and that this process, combined with a desire for technically sophisticated American equipment – which has turned Canadian "equipment envy" into another driving force – make the Americanization of the CF almost preordained. He adds that unification, by wiping out the traditional British counterbalance to American influence, hastened the process of Americanization which was largely completed by the budget cuts of the

Trudeau and Mulroney years. Granatstein concludes that if the CF ever abandon bilingualism, "there will be very little other than Canada's self-professed expertise in United Nation's peacekeeping to differentiate the military forces of the two countries."[1]

Lately, the trends toward Americanization that Granatstein observed may be accelerating. As a matter of policy over the next five years, the Department of National Defence (DND) intends to "manage our interoperability relationship with the US and other allies to permit seamless operational integration at short notice ... [to] develop a comprehensive program to adopt a new doctrine and equipment compatible with our principal allies ... [and to] expand the joint and combined exercise program to include all environments and exchanges with the US." A commitment has also been made to incorporate the application of concepts based on the Revolution in Military Affairs (RMA) into DND, especially in the realm of command and leadership. In part, this policy is based on the assumption that our closest neighbour "will in all likelihood remain the dominant global power."[2] The deliberate choice to embrace key tenets of the US armed forces' philosophy and doctrine by the senior leadership of DND is not a new phenomenon, but among the tendencies remarked upon since the Second World War. The Canadian military has been strongly influenced by one imperial power or another from the earliest days of organized armed forces in this country,[3] but DND's most recent intention to forge a closer relationship with the US armed services would, on the surface, suggest that the CF will become more "Americanized" in the years to come.

This book is a study of some of the major issues surrounding change and the associated Americanization of the CF since their unification in 1968. Some of the questions to be examined include these: How might such initiatives as the Revolution in Military Affairs, coalition operations, and the push toward interoperability with the US armed services affect the uniqueness of Canadian military doctrine and philosophy? Is it inevitable that American military values and ethics will be absorbed and internalized by Canadian officers, making it difficult for these officers to then embody and represent a uniquely Canadian military ethos? Is the Canadian officer corps at risk of being "Americanized"? And if this happens, what implications (both positive and negative) would it have for the Canadian Forces?

Many of these questions have been debated in various forms over the past thirty years, as commentators have asserted that the CF were going through a number of crises related to changes in Canadian society and the military. Whether these were crises of values, leadership, command, civil-military relations, ethos, ethics, or something else depended on the observer's perspective. In hindsight, perhaps it is fair to say that what the various critics were reacting to was the dimension of change in the CF they perceived to be most important. Rather than try to deal with any specific aspect of change, this study will rely on the overarching concept of culture to examine the various dimensions of change identified above and to attempt to account for not only their individual effects but also their cumulative effects on the CF.

Culture, described as the "bedrock of military effectiveness,"[4] has been selected as a unifying concept here because it can help explain the "motivations, aspirations, norms and rules of conduct" – what might be called the essence of the Canadian, or any other, military. The concept of culture also allows us to understand how new technologies may influence, and in turn be influenced by, military culture in the future. This is a crucial issue because we know that how armed forces fight may be "more a function of their culture than their doctrine" – or their technology for that matter.[5] History has shown that even when military forces have had access to the same technology, whether they developed the doctrine to use that technology effectively or not was largely a function of each force's culture.[6] As Paul Johnston put it, "formal doctrine is only one part of a military's character; so too are the experience and value systems of a military force's leaders; in fact, since armies choose doctrines, doctrines may be more a reflection of an organizational culture than a factor effecting change in the organizational culture."[7]

The ethos and ethics of a military organization are also closely linked to its culture, and a key part of that link is the officer corps as it bears the responsibility for creating and modifying the organizational culture of the military force as necessary. However, the ability of the officer corps to effect change in its force's organizational culture will always be constrained by certain factors, such as the armed forces' roles and the nature of the society in which the armed forces exist.

The concept of military culture is also important because it enables us to examine differences between services (e.g., army, navy, air force) and between units within the same service. These insights can help explain both the different approaches the services take to vital issues such as war fighting, leadership, and technology, and why various units may perform differently in roughly the same circumstances.

MILITARY CULTURE

Despite its utility in helping us to better understand change in the military, the concept of culture has its shortcomings. To date, many discussions of military culture have relied on James Burk's definition of the term, which includes his assertion that military culture is composed of four elements: discipline; professional ethos; ceremonial displays and etiquette; and cohesion and esprit de corps.[8] The analysis employed here recognizes Burk's definition but groups the three elements of discipline, ceremonial displays and etiquette, and cohesion and esprit de corps under the more inclusive topics of professional ethos and the relationship between the armed forces and society (sometimes expressed as civil-military relations): this approach is taken because these three of Burk's four elements are determined by a military force's professional ethos and the relationship the force has with its civil society.

Another problem with the existing literature, it has been argued, is that the vast amount of material that has been published under the rubric of military culture, especially in the US, "is not really about military culture at all." Snider argues that much of the debate in the press and academic literature on military culture is largely rhetorical and "focussed narrowly on the role of the traditional 'warrior' in military culture" as this role relates to the treatment of women, minorities, and homosexuals, and particularly in the US military. The analysis here aims to go beyond this largely sterile debate, by focusing on the essential issue of what is "distinctly *military* about military culture," in Snider's words. The framework used builds on the "functional" view that many aspects of military culture are derived from the roles and tasks armed services perform. But this discussion also embraces another approach, called "the heterogeneity of military culture" in examining the contributions of the subcultures of land, air, and maritime forces to a more general military culture.[9] Many of these areas have received very little attention from either the academic or professional military communities; therefore, the conclusions expressed here will be tentative and indicate where future research efforts could be directed. Finally, the discussion in this book has a land centric bias as most of the published research has focused on armies rather than navies or air forces.

APPROACH

The book begins, in this chapter, with an overview of the issues to be discussed later. Chapter 2 presents a summary of the theoretical approaches to culture. The discipline of organizational behaviour is the focus because it provides a multidisciplinary theoretical framework for discussing culture which allows a broad-based investigation into the key issues. The theoretical discussion of culture sets the stage for an investigation of military culture, in chapter 3, beginning with an examination of military professionals because they play a crucial role in shaping and reinforcing military culture. This chapter also explores two important factors in the debate on military culture – ethos and the relationship between the armed forces and society. Chapters 4 and 5 examine the American and the Canadian military cultures, in turn, with a view to understanding the roots of each culture and how each culture has coped with change since the Second World War. Topics of considerable debate and research in the US today – the civil-military gap and the relationship between the US armed forces and American society – are discussed in the section on American military culture. The chapter on Canadian military culture pays particular attention to the new ethos that has evolved since the unification of the Canadian armed forces and how this ethos compares to the traditional military ethos before unification. The cultures of the Canadian and American militaries are compared in chapter 6, with specific emphasis on the impact of contemporary Canadian civil society on these cultures, the nature of individual service cultures, and the influence of the new "joint" culture. The penultimate chapter looks at the future of Canadian and American military culture, considering the revolution in military affairs and operations other than war as potential influences on the development of these cultures. The book concludes with observations about how able the armed services of Canada and the US will be to cope with change and the challenges of the future.

In a recent essay, Colonel M.D. Capstick noted that those advising DND's senior leadership believe that the CF are in the midst of a period of "profound cultural change" and that a clear vision of "desired institutional culture" needs to be developed. However, there is little consensus on the definition of the desired CF culture, and Capstick wonders if it is even possible to develop a meaningful statement of one.[10] Clearly, the subject of Canadian military culture is critical to the institutional health of the CF, but it is still largely *terra incognita* and much remains to be done before we can have any comprehensive answers to the questions posed earlier. This book is an attempt to begin answering some of these questions by addressing some of the themes that follow.

The literature on military culture has grown rapidly over the past five years, but it has no clear focus. This book makes use of three representative theoretical constructs from the discipline of organizational behaviour in order to work toward a broader understanding of the concept of military culture in the North American context. Most writings on military culture come from the US, but this literature tends to be based on theories that emphasize the influence of strong cultures and leaders on organizational effectiveness. This book offers two other theoretical frameworks that may help account for ambiguity, conflict, and ethnic diversity in the military cultures of Canada and the US.

An important concept in the organizational behaviour literature is that of adaptive and non-adaptive cultures. The Canadian and American military cultures display some characteristics of non-adaptive cultures and may therefore be difficult to change in the future. The organizational behaviour literature also demonstrates that national cultures have a strong influence on organizational cultures; consequently, the Canadian and American armed services can be expected to be products of the societies from which they are drawn.

The profession of arms is another major theme in this study because it embodies the virtues and ethical norms that the military professionals – those with the legal and moral responsibility for deciding what aspects of military culture need to be changed and then effecting that change – should possess. The ethos of an armed force has a significant effect on its culture and way of doing things. A spirited debate continues in the US over the gap that is desirable or permissible between the military and the civilian ethos in a nation. In Canada this debate has largely focused on the degree of "civilianization" in the Canadian military, and whether this is good or bad. In general terms, the CF are more amenable to adopting societal norms than the American armed forces, which have argued that a larger gap is necessary between civil and military society in order to preserve the warrior ethos and combat effectiveness.

The various roles military forces perform are a defining element in shaping different military cultures. Whether between nations or between services, distinct roles produce distinct cultures. Based on this fact, the CF are in no immediate danger of losing their identity, but there are serious risks in pursuing interoperability with US forces, adopting US doctrine, and applying American RMA-based technical solutions to Canadian defence problems without considering how they might react with the culture of the CF.

This study therefore argues that the CF need to approach issues of interoperability and co-operation with US forces carefully, because American ways of doing things may not be compatible with Canadian military culture. Furthermore, the whole issue of the American Revolution in Military Affairs's potential effect on military culture needs to be carefully examined so that those technologies that are compatible with the Canadian military culture can be acquired in a timely fashion.

In the past the Canadian armed forces have played an illustrious role on the world stage. They have the potential to do so in the future, but the challenges of the twenty-first century must be met with a clear understanding of the essence of Canadian military culture and how it can best cope with necessary change. This study is a preliminary step in that direction.

2

Culture – "The Bedrock of Military Effectiveness"

Culture is a key concept for helping us to understand change in military organizations. Described as the "bedrock of military effectiveness" by the authors of a major report on American military culture in the twenty-first century,[1] military culture has recently become a focus of renewed scholarly interest in the armed services of various countries. The literature on military culture has grown rapidly over the past five years, and this literature is sprinkled with terms such as *values, attitudes*, and *beliefs*, and of course *culture* itself. Yet these concepts are rarely discussed in any detail. At best a succinct definition of the terms is found in some writings, but even then there are frequently somewhat different meanings assigned to them. This chapter will examine these and other relevant concepts in detail in an attempt to provide a consistent framework for answering the questions asked in the introduction.

Because members of a society or group derive most of their "motivations, aspirations, norms and rules of conduct" from the culture of that society or group, culture has considerable explanatory power in addressing the issues under discussion here. Most people accept that behaviour is influenced by culture, but describing the specific components of culture and understanding how they work can be a difficult task. One way of examining the impact of culture on the military is to use organizational culture as a construct which can explain how the "beliefs, norms, values, and premises" of members of the military govern their conduct.[2]

VALUES, ATTITUDES, BELIEFS, AND BEHAVIOUR

Before discussing the concept of culture, it is important to understand certain terms used repeatedly in the literature – *values, attitudes, beliefs,* and *behaviour.* The concepts these terms express are important to an analysis of any culture, including military culture, because they help us to understand how things work in a culture. A basic explanation of these concepts and the relationship between them follows. The more complex concepts of *culture* and *organizational culture* come later.

Values have been defined as "global beliefs that guide actions and judgements across a variety of situations."[3] The notion of values has been the subject of much debate in the organizational behaviour literature, but fundamentally values have the following characteristics.[4] Values are usually understood to be profound and relatively stable convictions that certain types of behaviour, courses of action, or outcomes are preferable to others. Values develop in the cultural setting in which they exist and have many sources, including parents, friends, teachers, and external reference groups. They often have a powerful effect on how leaders structure their organizations. For example, some people's value systems include the belief that subordinates are basically lazy and that if they are not closely supervised they will not work. This leads to a controlling organizational structure that can include time clocks, attendance boards, open concept offices where people can be observed constantly, and supervisors who are continually checking on their subordinates' work.

Some recent research on values suggests that North American workers are moving away from valuing economic incentives, organizational loyalty, and work-related identity toward valuing meaningful work, pursuit of leisure, personal identity, and self-fulfilment. This has important consequences for leaders today because it has been found that there is higher productivity among younger workers who are given jobs that match their values or who are supervised by people who share their values.[5]

Beliefs have been defined as "assumed facts about the world that do not involve evaluation." In this context, beliefs describe how certain concepts or ideas are perceived to fit together. Examples of beliefs range from the relatively concrete idea that "steel is hard" to more abstract notions such as "technology will improve our lives," "flexible work hours improve job satisfaction," or "close, directive supervision leads to higher productivity." Beliefs are learned not only through direct personal experience, like touching something made of steel, but also through indirect influences, such as advertising or the opinions of those a person respects. These indirect "social reinforcers" are among the most potent creators and reinforcers of beliefs.[6]

Attitudes have been defined as "a fairly stable emotional tendency to respond consistently to some object, situation, person, or category of people."[7] Attitudes have both a cognitive component (the opinions, beliefs, knowledge, or information a person possesses), and an emotional (or affective) component, usually involving the like or dislike of something and ordinarily related to the personal impact of that thing.[8] Attitudes are a product of a related belief and value. For example if you believe that flexible work hours improve job satisfaction (belief) and that high job satisfaction is good (value), then your attitude toward the work environment will likely be that flexible work hours are good (attitude). Attitudes are important because they often have a strong influence on behaviour. In the preceding example, if you are a supervisor who holds these views you might institute a flexible work routine among your subordinates.[9] The relationship between values, attitudes, beliefs, and behaviour is shown below.

VALUES + BELIEFS ⟶ ATTITUDES ⟶ BEHAVIOUR

Even though, in simple terms, attitudes are a product of values and beliefs, it is important to distinguish between the belief and value components of attitudes. For example, a supervisor observing poor performance among his/her subordinates might conclude that the group's behaviour (poor performance) is caused by "poor attitudes" toward high performance on the part of group members. However, in order to arrive at a clear understanding of the reasons behind the poor performance and to effect a desired change in the group's behaviour, the supervisor must distinguish between the belief and value components of attitudes. For example, the group might value high performance but believe that such performance is not achievable given the circumstances. Beliefs such as "we have not been adequately trained for this task," "our equipment is unreliable," or "this task is not important" might be behind the poor performance. On the other hand, the group might not value high performance in this situation if the values of some or all of the group's members are not congruent with those of the leader. For example, the leader might exhibit a very directive command style based on values that assume that his/her subordinates will not work effectively if they are not closely supervised. The leader's values could come into conflict with subordinates who value being allowed to achieve a task by exercising their initiative in a less structured environment. Attrition can also be partially explained by conflicting values. For example, if the organization's members value time with their families and organizational commitments preclude them having enough family time, some members may decide to leave the organization.[10]

Therefore, if leaders are to be effective in getting the desired behaviour from their subordinates, they must have a clear understanding of latter's values, attitudes, and beliefs. In the example given above, if beliefs appear to be limiting performance, then the basis for these beliefs (inadequate training, unreliable equipment, relevance of the task) will need to be carefully explored and addressed. On the other hand, if values appear to be the problem, then the leader may consider options such as changing group members in an attempt to achieve value congruence.[11]

Modifying attitudes has always been an important part of change in organizations. Until recently, it was believed that persuasion was the best way to modify the attitudes and beliefs of an organization's members. However, persuasion by itself has rarely been a successful method of effecting organizational change because members are often unable to see how new beliefs or attitudes will be applicable to their on-the-job behaviour. For example, soldiers may be told that women can be successfully integrated into combat arms units, but they may not understand how to apply this knowledge to actually dealing with women in their units. Another method – one which can be used in conjunction with persuasion – is teaching specific behaviours that can be used on the job and that correspond to the desired attitude change. It has been found that if personnel see that these behaviours are useful in carrying out their daily tasks then attitudes may change to correspond to the newly learned behaviours.[12] Change programs, however, should be designed as total packages. If attitudinal change is not reinforced by the organization's environment – for example, if some supervisors resist change or some co-workers ridicule the new behaviour – it may be very difficult to effect the desired change. Behaviours may instead revert to older forms or workers may rationalize the new behaviour without changing their attitudes.[13]

The preceding discussion is a simplified explanation of the relationship between values, attitudes, beliefs, and behaviour, and recent research has highlighted the tentative nature of the relationship between these factors.[14] Often an attitude results in intended behaviour but this behaviour may or may not be carried out, depending on the circumstances. For example, factors such as the existence of group norms, the degree of social pressure to conform to those norms, and whether or not a particular behaviour is perceived to have positive or negative consequences for the individual may all influence whether or not the behaviour is carried out. A recent high profile case involving Canadian troops in Croatia illustrates this point. Some members of a platoon expressed dissatisfaction with the platoon leader and openly discussed ways of "incapacitating" him; however, only a few apparently took any overt action by trying to "poison" him.[15]

ORGANIZATIONAL CULTURE

Most people think of culture as something related to exotic people far away, to strange myths, traditions, rituals, and food. In fact culture is far more than this. It is pervasive and critically important in understanding how all organizations work. While scholars from a number of different disciplines – notably anthropology, psychology, sociology, and organizational behaviour – have sparked a renaissance of interest in the topic, widely varying approaches to the subject have left the literature in a state of "conceptual chaos." There are advantages to multiple perspectives on culture, not least of which is a broader view as the subject is too complex to be adequately covered by any one outlook. It must also be realized that there is a certain subjectivity even in "scientific" approaches to studying culture, as the background, gender, and education of researchers affect how they select what is important for them to observe in an organizational culture and how they interpret what they observe. For example, many in the United States might interpret the term *race* to imply the social construct of the black-white dichotomy often used to classify people in that country by their skin colour.[16] In Canada, while some have adopted a similar construct, others might use the term *race* in the context of Canada's two "founding races," where the notion of race is based primarily on the linguistic and cultural differences between French- and English-speaking Canadians.

The term *culture* was first defined in the social sciences over 125 years ago, and today as many as 250 definitions exist.[17] Commentators acknowledge that no generally accepted definition of culture, let alone organizational culture, exists.[18] Nevertheless, there is some consensus on certain aspects of organizational culture, for example that there are several layers of culture and that each level differs in its visibility and resistance to change.[19] The discipline of anthropology has one of the most inclusive concepts of culture, seeing it as all aspects of a group's behaviour and social organization. Anthropologists investigate, interpret, and translate the behaviour and social patterns of foreign cultures in order to make them intelligible to us.[20]

In the discipline of organizational behaviour, culture is often seen as the collection of values, attitudes, and beliefs which provide people with a common way of interpreting events.[21] Sharing the broad perspective of the traditional anthropological model, this discipline views organizations as social entities composed of human beings which create systems of meanings that influence behaviour and develop routines and practices which are recognized as a distinct way of organizational life. In this context, culture can be defined as a learned way of coping with the challenges of life. As long as the organization's coping strategies are effective, its culture keeps the organization together by establishing a common framework of reference and interpretation for its members which enables them to deal with internal and external challenges.[22] Culture is a very useful concept in this setting because it helps us explain some of the seemingly incomprehensible and irrational aspects of groups and organizations.[23]

Because it is based on such disciplines as psychology, sociology, political science, economics, anthropology, and history, the field of organizational behaviour provides a multidisciplinary theoretical framework for discussing culture. The organizational behaviour approach is also useful because no organization exists in isolation. All organizations, particularly military institutions, exist within other structures, such as economies, societies, and nation states or other political entities. Organizational behaviour's multidisciplinary approach provides a wider perspective on culture than can be had from the literature of one discipline; this is why it will be used here as the principal theoretical approach.[24]

Just over fifteen years ago, organizations were usually thought of as rational agents for co-ordinating and controlling a group of people.[25] This assumption began to change in the mid-1980s, when a wave of literature on organizational culture started to appear.[26] This new literature argued that organizational culture serves four basic functions. First, it provides an organization's members a sense of identity and increases their commitment to the organization. If they internalize organizational values, they can find their work intrinsically rewarding and be more highly motivated. Next, culture helps members make sense of or interpret the meaning of organizational events. Third, culture reinforces the values held in the organization. Finally, culture serves as a control mechanism, with norms that guide behaviour and shape behaviour.[27]

This study considers three representative frameworks for interpreting organizational culture. The selection of theoretical frameworks is not intended to be comprehensive, but to give the reader a sense of the major approaches to organizational culture that might help answer the questions posed at the beginning of the book. The first framework is based on the work of one of the earliest researchers in organizational culture, Edgar H. Schein. His work has been used as the starting point for much subsequent work on the subject in the West, and he is one of the few who has tried to establish a coherent framework for the study of organizational behaviour. His work has been critiziced, however, and later in this section important challenges to Schein's constructs by Jesper S. Pedersen and Jesper S. Sorensen will be examined as they help interpret some aspects of military culture that Schein's theories do not explain adequately. The third framework that will be described is organizational behaviour in its international and multicultural dimensions as articulated by Diana

Pheysey. This approach, although not yet widely used in the literature on military culture, will become increasingly relevant to Canadian military professionals both from the perspective of multinational operations and, perhaps more importantly, from the perspective of this country's changing demographics due to immigration.

Schein tells us that the concept of organizational culture allows leaders to understand how organizational learning occurs.[28] He also maintains that development and planned change within an organization cannot be understood without considering the culture and subcultures that exist in the organization. A prime source of resistance to change, because it is a stabilizing force in human systems, culture is one of the most difficult aspects to manage in a climate of perpetual change. According to Schein, the concept of organizational culture has great explanatory power. Many problems which were once viewed as communications failures or as resulting from a lack of teamwork are now more properly understood as breakdowns of intercultural communications. In fact, achieving organizational integration requires understanding subcultures and designing intergroup processes to allow communication and collaboration across sometimes strong subcultural boundaries. These processes might include activities like social events or sports competitions where groups representing various subcultures interact. Or, the processes could include formal structures, such as committees which give representatives from various subcultures a forum in which to exchange views. The concept of organizational culture also allows us to understand how new technologies influence and are influenced by organizations, because, as will be seen later, human responses to technology are often critical to the integration of technology into an organization.[29]

Leadership, according to Schein, is also an integral part of organizational culture, because cultures begin with leaders who impose their values and assumptions on a group. However, once a culture takes root, it will define for future generations of members the kinds of leadership that are acceptable to it. While Schein acknowledges that culture is just one element of a complex group of learning processes only partially influenced by leader behaviour, he claims that the creation, evolution, and management of culture ultimately define leadership, and that one of the most decisive functions of leadership is the creation, management, and sometimes the destruction of culture. The role of a leader in the life of an organization varies. In a group's formative stages the members' anxiety is typically high, and leadership is actively sought by the group. In this case, organizational culture tends to be a positive growth force which needs to be elaborated, developed and articulated; the leader plays a key role in this process. In the middle period of an organization's existence, culture becomes diverse since many subcultures will have formed. Deciding what elements need to be changed then becomes a tough and strategic issue for leaders. In an organization's maturity and decline stages, culture is often partially dysfunctional and can only be changed through more drastic processes such as scandals and turnarounds.[30]

Based on these precepts, Schein defines organizational culture as, "A pattern of shared assumptions that the group learned as it solved its problems of external adaptation and internal integration, that worked well enough to be considered valid and, therefore, to be taught to new members as the correct way to perceive, think, and feel in relation to these problems."[31]

When it was first proposed, this definition introduced three elements not previously discussed in the literature. The first element was the issue of socialization, or what is passed on to new members. Schein reminds us that only surface aspects of culture are part of the socialization process, and that the heart of a culture is only revealed to those who enter the group's inner circles. The second issue relates to behaviour. This definition does not include overt behaviour patterns, because they are determined by cultural predisposition and situational contingencies from the environment and they do not necessarily tell us anything about deeper cultural assumptions. The third element relates to Schein's assertion that subcultures can form within certain organizations.[32]

Schein raises the key concept of the various levels at which organizational culture exists. He posits three levels of culture: artifacts, espoused values, and basic assumptions.

Artifacts are visible organizational structures and processes which, being on the surface, are easy to observe but often difficult to decipher. Organization charts, committee structures, standard operating procedures, and military doctrine are examples of artifacts that can often be easily observed. However, if taken at face value these cultural artifacts can give a deceptive picture of the organization. For example, as Johnston noted, armed forces do not always follow their written doctrine; drawing conclusions about how a military force fights based on published doctrine could therefore be misleading.[33]

Values comprise the next, deeper, level of culture.[34] Espoused values are conscious, articulated values that are primarily normative statements which reflect attitudes, hopes, or beliefs about how people would like things to be as opposed to how they really are.[35] The "golden rule" of "Do unto others as you would have them do unto you" has been given as an example of a value statement that is widely espoused but not widely practiced.[36] Espoused values predict reasonably well what people will *say* in a variety of situations but may not reflect what they will actually *do* in situations where those values should be operating. This is particularly true if espoused values are rationalizations or aspirations for the future. However, according to Schein, if espoused values are congruent with underlying assumptions, then articulation of these values can foster group cohesion.

In this model, basic assumptions, are the deepest and most fundamental level of an organization's culture.[37] Basic assumptions are so taken for granted that one finds little variation in a cultural unit. These implicit, unconscious assumptions often deal with fundamental aspects of life (e.g., our interpretation of human nature or the importance of work and family). Because of their pervasiveness, basic assumptions are almost never confronted nor debated within the group, and they are extremely difficult to change. Nevertheless, to predict a group's future behaviour it is crucial to understand the group's basic assumptions. This is true because "rather than tolerate anxiety, we tend to perceive events around us as congruent with our assumptions even if it means distorting, denying, or projecting or otherwise falsifying what is going on around us."[38] Basic assumptions, in other words, provide us with a mental map or framework to help us interpret events in a way that reduces anxiety or stress.

According to Schein, the essence of a group's culture is its pattern of shared, taken-for-granted basic assumptions – its cultural paradigm. This paradigm is described as an interlocking, coordinated set of assumptions. Taken individually, each assumption explains little; it is their pattern together which explains the behaviour and success of an organization in overcoming external and internal challenges. The cultural paradigm is manifest in observable artifacts, shared espoused values, norms, and rules of behaviour. Schein asserts that in order to interpret cultural artifacts correctly or to know how much credence should be given to articulated values one must decipher the pattern of basic assumptions that may be operating in the organization.[39]

Being so pervasive in the literature, Schein's interpretations will appear most frequently in this book; however, his work has its limitations. Pedersen and Sorensen build on Schein's work but offer some different insights into organizational culture. Their interpretation will be used when it offers a better picture of how humans behave in organizations.

Pedersen and Sorensen observed that organizations are often dominated by differentiation, inconsistency, ambiguity, and conflict instead of a dominant, cohesive culture. They found organizations with varied subcultures and lacking a significant corporate culture. Members of subcultures often acted on the basis of numerous internally consistent values which caused conflict with other subcultural units. They also observed important differences between cultural value systems among occupations, resulting in subcultures with different goals, and some directly opposed to each other, thus causing severe problems in co-operation and co-ordination within an organization.[40] According to long-time Pentagon reporter Arthur Hadley, a situation of this sort exists in the US military. In his book *The Straw Giant*, he maintained that, because of the different roles and missions of the services, conflicting subcultures have long been a part of the American military culture. Since Army officers work in a close-knit team with teams of others in combat, the officers are more conscious of the needs of others and more supportive of teamwork than the officers of other services. Hadley claims that naval officers have an independence of operation, a sense of isolation from other parts of the defence world bred into them that shows up as a tendency to fight "joint" assignments, to downgrade shore postings, and to avoid courses for professional development. Finally, Air Force officers, removed from the effects of combat compared to Army officers, tend to embrace technical solutions to problems, which fosters a "strong strain of anti-intellectualism" among them.[41] These assumptions and their possible effects on American military culture will be examined in more detail later.

Pedersen and Sorensen are particularly critical of Schein's claim that the cultural paradigm is the essence of an organization's culture. They interpret the paradigm as an ambiguous system reflecting the cultural realities of coexisting, interdependent, and logically contradictory cultural assumptions which may have occupational, class, ethnic, or geographic origins. Pedersen and Sorensen believe that the concept of basic assumptions and a coherent cultural paradigm are the result of analysts' attempts to create an orderly world where none exists. They see Schein's category of "basic assumptions" not as the essence of culture but as an analytical tool constructed by researchers in the field. In Pedersen and Sorensen's view, an organization may operate from some kind of base but it need not be coherent, consistent, and rational. They distinguish between espoused values and what they term "values-in-use," which actually function as guidelines for behaviour in an organization. They also claim that empirical research suggests that espoused values and values-in-use are not tightly coupled. This may be due largely to the fact that espoused values often address an external audience, and while they may be promulgated widely and almost everyone claims to agree with them, they do not necessarily have any impact on the behaviour of members of an organization, because espoused values exist for purposes of legitimization and image building.[42] Furthermore, it may be that members of the organization never change their individual culture; rather, it is the organization that may change its culture by adding new functions and occupations – and consequently members with different cultures – or by replacing older generations in the organization with newer generations. This replacement process changes the values and patterns of basic assumptions in an organization.[43]

THE LEADER'S ROLE IN SHAPING CULTURE

According to Schein, leaders play crucial roles in shaping and reinforcing culture. Leaders influence how an organizational culture develops based on what they focus on. They communicate their values, priorities, and beliefs through what they notice, comment on, measure, and control. Modelling, teaching, coaching, and mentoring are powerful tools for shaping culture, and their messages are amplified in times of crisis. If leaders are consistent in what they pay attention to, members receive clear signals about what is important in the organization. In contrast, inconsistent signals spread confusion as members spend a lot of time trying to decipher and find meaning in erratic leader behaviour. Subordinates look to leaders for cues to appropriate behaviour and often emulate leader behaviour. How leaders allocate rewards in an organization also has a strong influence on organizational culture, but, to be effective, leaders should reward behaviour that is consistent with values. This is not always the case. For example, some organizations, like militaries, claim to value teamwork but base promotion on individual performance ratings. This can send confusing signals to members. The recruiting and selection of new members also send a message to members of the organization. Current military recruiting policies not only influence the organization's composition but also send messages to members about what type of person is valued. Another related factor is the treatment of members who are perceived as performing poorly. Relocating poor performers in the organization sends one message; firing them sends another. In all the activities described above, leaders model the ethical norms that help to regulate member behaviour, and this also has a profound effect on an organizational culture.[44]

The actions of leaders, sometimes classed as artifacts of an organizational culture, constitute another powerful tool for communicating with members of the organization. Formal ceremonies and rites, such as the presentation of awards and medals in the military, are ways of sending messages to members about organizational values. Rituals are everyday organizational practices that send a clear message about "the way things are done" in an organization. For example, the use of first names in an organization, versus ranks or titles, may tell us about power distance in the organization.[45] The differences in this regard are evident in the way titles and names are used in the army, navy, and air force. For example, in the Canadian Army a Master Warrant Officer (MWO) will usually be addressed as Sergeant-Major by his superior, whereas in the air force the superior might address the MWO by his/her first name. Leaders can also use symbols, like headdress (berets versus wedge caps for example) to communicate organizational culture by unspoken messages. Stories are another way to give meaning to activities that occur in the organization and they can be a potent communications tool when listeners are left to draw their own conclusions. However, stories that are not congruent with reality can lead to cynicism and mistrust.[46]

Socialization is a key method of cultural communication in an organization. The primary purpose of socialization is to transmit core values to newcomers through training, interaction with role models, and the newcomers' observation of the types of behaviour that are rewarded and punished. Newcomers are vigilant observers and if socialization is to be effective, it is essential that the messages given during the socialization process reflect the underlying values of the organization. While information about cultural artifacts and espoused values is relatively easy to convey to newcomers; communicating values-in-use is more difficult and the organization's basic assumptions are almost impossible to convey accurately.[47] More recently the tendency to use the socialization process to assimilate newcomers has been replaced with the process of integration. This process allows people who come from diverse backgrounds to retain important aspects of their identity and culture while still joining the group.[48]

CHANGING AN ORGANIZATIONAL CULTURE

Changing an organization's culture is feasible but difficult, because assumptions, the deepest level of culture, are unconscious, "nonconfrontable and nondebatable."[49] Another reason culture is hard to change is that it is often deeply ingrained and behavioural norms are well learned; therefore, members must unlearn the old norms before they can learn new ones. Several actions can be taken to modify organizational culture. The first is to change behaviour in the organization, but this is not enough on its own because behaviour is only an artifact of culture. Another action, cultural communication, is extremely important, but it is crucial that the communication be credible and that leaders live the new values and not just talk about them. The recruiting and selection process can also be used to alter organizational culture. Selection strategies can be devised to pick those individuals who more accurately reflect the desired culture, and those who resist change can be encouraged to leave. But changing personnel in an organization is normally a lengthy process that cannot be accomplished effectively in a short period of time. Cultural change can be assumed to be successful if the new behaviour becomes intrinsically motivated and persists even if certain rewards are not present. Successful organizations promote a culture that empowers members to exercise their creativity and productivity in achieving the organization's goals, but this often requires eliminating traditional hierarchical notions of power.[50]

Schein's work tends to be based on the framework of Western, particularly North American, culture. Diana Pheysey's writings combine the concepts of national culture and organizational culture, and are therefore vital to understanding military culture in an international or multicultural setting. Her ideas are explored in the next section.

NATIONAL CULTURE AND ORGANIZATIONAL CULTURE

A society's culture is expressed not just in its art, language, and food, but also in how it solves its survival problems and deals with the daily challenges of life. There are identifiable differences among how different cultures interpret events. For example, in Western cultures people tend to think that a cause precedes an effect or that an event has an identifiable cause or causes and that events happen sequentially, one after the other, in a linear chain of events. People in Eastern cultures tend to perceive life as more of a two-way interaction between events. In other words, the relationship between events is more circular in nature, with one event causing another event, but the second event then interacts with the first to modify it.[51] War itself, despite attempts by Western militaries to fit it into a linear, Newtonian model, may best be interpreted using the Eastern cultural paradigm to explain unpredictability, uncertainty, and the non-linear nature of the modern battlefield.[52]

Even the thought processes of people from Western and Eastern cultures are different. People with a Western cultural outlook tend to interpret reality as being based on science and pragmatism, whereas those with an Eastern cultural outlook tend to see reality as based more on revealed truth than empirical experimentation; the latter therefore have a greater regard for intuition than many raised in the Western tradition.[53] The Western regard for empiricism may be overstated, however, by those with a vested interest in promoting that paradigm. Canada's second Nobel Laureate in physics, Bertram Brockhouse, was described by a colleague as having "this gift of just knowing what the answer is, then doing the experiment to prove it."[54] This is not exactly the epitome of Western empiricism – in fact it seems much closer to the Oriental intuitive method.

Researchers in the field of organizational behaviour have found that cultural values influence behaviour in organizations. For example, in countries like Indonesia, the Philippines, and Nigeria, people with high status (such as military officers) are regarded with awe and are thought to have the right to exercise control over many aspects of their subordinates' work and lives, whereas, in Singapore, Taiwan, and Kenya, people expect organizations to provide opportunities for friendship, sharing, and involvement in workplace decisions, and leaders are expected to respect these desires. A key finding in organizational behaviour cross-cultural research is that employees of the same companies hold values that are strongly influenced by their national culture. This implies that leaders must use different approaches to reach the same goals in multinational organizations, depending on the national cultures involved. It was found, however, that irrespective of the culture, anytime "coercive power" is used, it tends to alienate those subjected to it and to make them angry or frightened.[55]

Pheysey has proposed four general types of national culture based on a circular continuum, with the circularity reflecting the fact that societies evolve and change, moving around the continuum. Pheysey describes these four cultures as (1) law-abiding societies that try to reduce uncertainty in their members by regulating behaviour with laws and codes of conduct, (2) economically competitive societies where individualism is prized, (3) harmonious societies where co-operation and the minimization of conflict are valued, and (4) powerfully led societies where strong leaders are given wide scope to direct the individuals' activities. Based on the same methodology, Pheysey also hypothesizes that four general types of organizational culture exist: (1) role cultures, which are often large, hierarchical organizations where conformity to superiors' expectations based on a clear articulation of jobs and procedures is emphasized; (2) achievement cultures, where people resolve their own problems and satisfy their own needs and expectations because they find the work itself challenging and a source of motivation; (3) support cultures, where all individuals participate in the decision-making process and it is assumed that people will contribute to organizational goals out of a sense of commitment to the group, which provides them with emotional and physical support; and (4) power cultures, where strong people with high status direct the activities of subordinates who are expected to be compliant and willing. Pheysey emphasizes that these models are not meant to be overly prescriptive, because cultures vary in strength and evolve over time. Additionally, while national cultures influence organizational cultures, organizational cultures in turn may induce change in national cultures.[56]

Pheysey's work offers a powerful critique of those organizational behaviour theories that are based on Maslow's hierarchy of needs, which posits that humans tend to fulfill their needs in a sequential, hierarchical way, starting with basic physical needs and progressing up to the highest need of self-actualization. For example, in support organizations, social (belonging) needs – in the middle of Maslow's hierarchy – may be the most basic because belonging to a group is the only way to meet physical needs adequately. In addition, different cultures might not interpret Maslow's needs in the same way. Pheysey claims that the individualism implicit in "self-actualization" in a Western context might be completely foreign in an Eastern context.[57] Her work also provides fresh insights into how organizations in different cultures achieve the degree of control they need in order to function effectively.

CONTROL IN CULTURES

All organizations attempt to control[58] internal and external events and overcome obstacles to reaching their goals. Role cultures, common in many military organizations, tend to control by regulation or plan.[59] Commanders and their staffs devise plans which are executed by officers – persons described as "office holders" in civilian organizations.[60] The work of the officers is monitored by superiors who adjust the plan as necessary. In role cultures, procedures for meeting difficulties are largely routinized, and in military cultures this is epitomized by vast amounts of published doctrine and regulations. In power cultures, there is a greater reliance on supervision as a means of ensuring that plans are implemented as desired; however, since plans may not be written down, subordinates may have to appeal to a superior for guidance before initiating corrective action. In both role and power cultures, planning precedes execution, and the people doing the work are expected to comply with the instructions of their superiors.[61]

In achievement and support cultures, the preferred method of control is control by appreciation. In this context, appreciation means what is noticed, how it is classified, and the way it is valued. In achievement and support cultures, planning and execution tend to be done concurrently and to be carried out by the same people. Execution is normally given to "autonomous work groups" which are allowed to exercise their own judgment in the completion of tasks. Often employees are professionals who have been specially trained to exercise their judgment, and responsibility for the quality of the work therefore rests with the person doing the job, not someone else. Pheysey claims that regulative control is linked to Western concepts of rationality and that appreciation is linked with Eastern ways of thinking.[62] Many students of military history, however, know that the German concept of *Auftragstaktik* (or "mission tactics") – a command method introduced in the nineteenth century by the German Army stressing initiative in battle at all levels right down to individual soldiers – shows that even a stereotypically "rational" and rigid organization can value initiative.[63]

In practice all organizations need to use both the role and appreciation types of control, but each type of organization responds better to one type than the other.[64] Each method of control has its advantages and disadvantages. Regulation often encourages people "to make the numbers look good," sometimes collecting evidence to cover themselves when the figures cannot be made to look good. The "body count" example from the Vietnam conflict is a striking example of the weaknesses of control by regulation. The US government's insistence on hard data from the field to be subjected to computer-driven, rational cost-benefit analysis resulted in troops in the field being rewarded on the basis of the number of enemy killed. By the autumn of 1967, the command system was faced with multiple, systematic falsifications of data in response to the needs of a management process based on regulation.[65] This type of control can result in both a loss of useful, even critical, information and in leaders' unwillingness to take risks. On the other hand, with control by appreciation, leaders have little control over the actual behaviour of subordinates, goals may be difficult to assess, and some employees will not respond to the responsibility that appreciative control gives them. When used appropriately, however, appreciative control can lead to better problem-solving capabilities and higher worker motivation.[66]

In role and power cultures, leaders tend to believe that people are naturally lazy, and therefore that their behaviour has to be shaped by rewards or sanctions. This is often referred to as extrinsic motivation. Appreciation cultures tend to use intrinsic motivation more frequently. One problem with using only extrinsic rewards on those who value intrinsic motivators is that if they are treated like irresponsible, lazy people, they may begin to act accordingly. The literature today endorses the view that if people are to fulfill their potential they must be encouraged to take responsibility for what they do.[67]

In a seminal article on the impact of policies on military values and cultures, William F. Bell, a lieutenant-colonel in the US Army, summarizes some of the key theoretical issues regarding organizational behaviour that will later be applied to an analysis of American and Canadian military culture. Basing his analysis on Schein's theories, Bell notes that policies in all organizations can create a gap between an organization's stated and espoused values on one hand and its actual or operational values on the other hand, what Pedersen and Sorensen called values-in-use. When this gap appears, it is often because policies tend to be developed in isolation, for their own purposes, and without considering the effects the policies might have on organizational values. Furthermore, in large organizations like armed forces, the people who develop policy are rarely those who have to implement it, due to both a functional separation between administrators and operators and a rapid turnover due to "career-enhancing" postings.

Bell argues that when policies have negative effects on organizational culture it is usually because of unintended second and third order consequences. Unfortunately, by the time the senior leadership becomes aware of the unintended effects, a substantial portion of the organization has adjusted to a new cultural paradigm caused by the unintended second and third order consequences. At the point when senior leadership owes its success to the new value-in-use paradigm, internal change becomes highly improbable. Like tends to promote like in the officer hierarchy, and change back to stated values is no longer possible without external impetus. If the new value-in-use paradigm is left in place for any length of time, it will change organizational culture. All organizations suffer from the unintended consequences of policies, according to Bell, and it is impossible to avoid them. However, to minimize the unintended consequences' negative effects, feedback mechanisms must be in place to track the implementation of individual policies and to continually gauge the "value health" of the organization.

In this model, all policies should be evaluated according to three criteria: (1) Did the policy achieve the desired end? (2) Does the policy reinforce the values of the organization? and (3) Does the policy work in conjunction with other policies to further the ends of the organization? As Schein implied, leaders must manage the organizational culture or the culture will manage them.

Naturally, any challenge to the status quo will cause anxiety and defensiveness, but, Bell argues, the fundamental role of the leader is to do exactly that. Bell differentiates between managers and leaders, using Schein's model, in asserting that managers are controlled by existing organizational values while leaders shape, create, and change the organization's values to develop the culture the organization requires.[68]

The term *organizational climate*, "how members of an organization feel about the organization," has been used to describe an observable and measurable artifact of organizational culture. Organizational climate is "more malleable and responsive to immediate pressures and policy guidance" than organizational culture, but organizational climate can have a major impact on underlying culture over the long term. While organizational climate can be altered in the near term, changes are largely limited to those aspects of the organizational environment that members are aware of, and not the deeper, implied values that underlie organizational culture. Factors that influence organizational climate include perceptions about the system of rewards and punishments, the flow of information up and down the organizational hierarchy, expectations about job performance, the fairness of the administrative system, characteristics of the work, and the example set by leaders.[69] Organizational climate and culture are related in complex ways that are not clearly understood.[70]

CULTURE AND PERFORMANCE

The effects of organizational culture on performance have been hotly debated, but, because it is difficult to quantify many of the effects, the debate continues. Some believe, for example, that strong organizational cultures improve performance, but research demonstrates only a moderate correlation between strong organizational culture and performance.[71] On one hand, strong cultures create predictability, orderliness, and consistency without the need for extensive written rules and regulations. On the other hand, by demanding conformity, strong cultures can limit the range of values and styles of behaviour that are acceptable and can even undermine formal diversity policies.[72] Another perspective on organizational culture, the "fit" perspective, argues that a particular culture is only appropriate for an organization if it fits the organization's strategy. The environment, requirements, and societal expectations are factors that may help to explain whether or not a culture is a good fit for an organization. For example, the complex hierarchy found in military headquarters may not be appropriate for field units who must react quickly to a complex and changing situation. According to research, the fit perspective helps to explain short-term performance but not long-term performance in an organization. A third approach to culture and performance is the adaptation perspective. It holds that only cultures that help organizations adapt to environmental change are associated with excellent performance. An adaptive culture encourages confidence and risk-taking among members and focuses on the changing needs of its stakeholders. Leaders pay close attention to all their constituencies and initiate change when required. Non-adaptive cultures are characterized by cautious leaders who try to protect their own interests, often by behaving insularly, politically, and bureaucratically. They tend to value orderly and risk-reducing management processes much more highly than leadership initiatives.[73] As we shall see later, the US and Canadian armed forces exhibit many of the characteristics of non-adaptive cultures.

This summary of the theoretical approaches to culture sets the stage for an investigation of military culture, beginning with an examination of military professionals as the "ultimate keepers"of military culture.[74] The rest of this chapter examines the profession of arms as the source of many facets of military culture.

ORIGINS OF THE PROFESSION OF ARMS AND MODERN MILITARY CULTURE

The idea that war fighting required a specialized body of knowledge or theories is relatively new, dating from the late eighteenth century, but it is now universally accepted.[75] During the nineteenth century the profession of arms was one of many new professions that emerged in Western societies. Like the other new professions, it sought to make its expertise "scientific" and the exclusive preserve of practitioners of the profession – the military officers.[76] Improved selection, education, and promotion of officers made the armed services increasingly distinct from the civilian world and from the traditional identification of the role of the officer with the aristocracy or upper classes. Today the military forces of the West are wrestling with the same issues of competence, service to society, and ethical behaviour that the older professions, like medicine and the law, are grappling with. The debate has taken on new urgency with various commissions of inquiry looking into the performance of the profession of arms. In Canada, the Somalia Commission set in train a whole series of reforms aimed at improving the profession of arms in this country, and yet not everyone accepts that the proposed reforms have improved the state of the profession here. An understanding of the nature of the profession of arms is crucial to being able to evaluate the state of the Canadian officer corps both now and in the future.

The idea of a profession is based on groups of people who have a monopoly on certain skills for a "distinct practical purpose." Barzun reminds us that this focus on practicality means that professions are vulnerable to change, because, while the general functions of professions may be eternal, a particular profession may disappear or change radically over time. He uses the examples of the priest-physician and barber-surgeon to illustrate this point, and he notes that the "tendency of an egalitarian age to turn every occupation into a profession" has complicated the subject of professional ethics. He uses the example of the "profession" of journalism to demonstrate that the term professional is frequently used incorrectly. In the case of journalists, there is no body of peers to judge if practitioners are competent, the "professional" has a distant relationship with his/her clients, and there are no specific professional credentials required to become a journalist. Therefore, journalists could be said to meet few of the criteria of a true profession. This trend to raise occupations to professional status is paralleled by the gradual demoting of some professions, including the military profession, to the level of ordinary trades. Barzun asserts that for professions to survive they must recover their mental and moral force. It is not enough to have codes of conduct that are policed by professional oversight bodies; professions must also have "moral and intellectual leadership" that communicates the message that ethical behaviour is "desirable, widely practiced, approved and admired."[77] Or as Lerner puts it, all professions need to "recapture the sense of vocation or calling."[78]

There is some debate over whether service in the armed forces constitutes a profession or not. One of the most pervasive descriptions of officership as a profession is the one given by the distinguished American scholar Samuel Huntington in 1957.[79] Much of the Western literature on military professionalism is suffused with Huntington's ideas and vocabulary. While his model, though dominant in the literature on military professionalism, has been criticized by a number of writers, the essence of Huntington's views on professionalism have been endorsed by senior DND leaders.[80] Huntington explained that the three defining characteristics of a profession are expertise, responsibility, and corporateness. Expertise is specialized knowledge acquired only by prolonged education and experience. Essential to maintaining this expertise is continual study and practice of the profession. The professional also has a responsibility to practice his/her profession in the service of society; the profession therefore holds certain moral principles in dealing with laypersons. Finally, professionals share a sense of unity among themselves and separateness from those who are not members of their profession, partly because of the lengthy training necessary to achieve professional competence.

The military profession lays claim to the expertise of the application of violence by a military force in the service of the state. But unlike police officers and firefighters, who are often compared to military professionals because they risk their lives in the service of society and, in the case of police, are authorized to use deadly force in some circumstances, soldiers go to their work with the deliberate intention of destroying lives and property. As Bercuson points out, however, military professionals are trained for war, not to have a "killer mentality."[81] According to Huntington, the duties of military officers as professionals therefore include (1) the organizing, equipping, and training of military forces; (2) the planning of their activities; and (3) the direction of their operation in and out of combat. Modern military forces also contain many types of specialists, but only those who "manage violence" are true military professionals. Others, such as doctors, dentists, lawyers, and pharmacists, may have expertise that is necessary for the military force to achieve its objectives, but they are not competent to manage violence. As Huntington puts it, they belong to the officer corps in an administrative capacity but are not part of the professional body of the officer corps. This is understandable because most of these specialists are trained in their own professional schools (e.g., medical schools) and serve only a small part of their career in the military, usually returning to practice their profession in a civilian setting.

Like many Western armed forces, the CF believe that some of its members, particularly the officers, practice a profession, and the CF therefore promote the idea that a military career is not just a job but a vocation or way of life. Members of the CF are expected to possess military virtues and rely on them to perform beyond what is expected of their civilian counterparts. Some in Canada believe that the CF should serve "as a symbol of all that is best in the national character." However, the Somalia Commission concluded that military professionalism in Canada has been undermined by "a shift toward 'civilianization.'" This has resulted in the infusion of occupational values in the CF, versus the traditional vocational values. The influence of technology, which has forced increased specialization and civilian skills onto Western armed services, plus the reorganization of the CF in the 1960s and 1970s have exacerbated this trend. The Somalia Commission, citing Cotton, argued that "military service as a calling or vocation, made legitimate by broadly based national values, had given way to" a perception that those in the military were performing civilian type jobs for rewards specified under contracts often seen in the business sector. According to Owen Parker, this has led to reduced standards of accountability among senior officers, who are now unwilling to accept responsibility when things go wrong in their command.[82] These issues will be examined in more detail when Canadian military culture is discussed.

In 1972, Abrahamsson provided a thorough critique of professionalism as a model to explain the functions of the officer corps. He argued that like all organizations, armed services are concerned with growth, improvement, and their own survival. He contended that they should be seen for what they really are, not disinterested professionals, but a politicized, highly active interest group that holds strong political views. Of course these characteristics could also be ascribed to many other professional groups that lobby governments for resources to support their activities. Perlmutter's 1977 "fusionist" model holds that all states are to some degree praetorian as professional military officers are drawn into national policy-making even in "advanced" Western states. For Perlmutter, the key to the interaction between the armed services and the state is that modern armed services are distinguished by their corporate professionalism. As corporate entities, they work to maintain their existence and protect their exclusivity. Perlmutter proposed three broad categories of armed services: (1) the professional corporate, found mostly in Western liberal democracies; (2) the praetorian, found in those states where civilian authority is weak; and (3) the revolutionary, found where there is a strong ideological component which encompasses the whole of society.[83]

THE PROFESSION OF ARMS IN CANADA

Most of the literature supports the notion of the Canadian Forces as a professional corporate body. Like other professions in Canada, the profession of arms controls the "education, training, and socialization of its members" with its own institutions, including schools and colleges. The CF do not have a standard ethical code, but officers "freely enter into a moral and legal contract that imposes professional duties and standards" based on the texts of their commissions and oaths. The Oath of Allegiance is the Canadian service person's "code of moral obligation."[84] However, unlike other professions in Canadian society, the military can be called upon to ensure the very survival of the nation. In executing this function, as well as other military roles, members of the military can be called upon to lay down their lives – sometimes expressed as the concept of unlimited liability. Another distinction between the military professional and other professionals is that military leaders have the right to sacrifice the lives of their subordinates in order to achieve military objectives.

Many things have affected the professionalism of the Canadian officers corps in the past. Perhaps the most significant event, according to Bland, was the fusion of the military staff of Canadian Forces Headquarters with the public service staff of the Department of National Defence in 1972 to create National Defence Headquarters. This had a significant impact on the professionalism of the officer corps because it "blurred and then distorted the chain of command and accountability in the armed forces." The new roles that some senior officers played in DND after 1972 left them confused about their true role as military professionals. Some accepted that "they had a responsibility to protect the minister and the government from criticism which is a short step to acting in a partisan political manner," Bland claims. He also argues that a consequence of this role confusion was that "civil control of the armed forces was compromised, military advice was buried in efforts to forge bureaucratic collegiality, and some officers in the headquarters lost touch with the operational and human needs of the Canadian Forces." Only recently has the Canadian public become aware of these problems, leading a number of commentators to claim that the "erosion of the military ethos allowed a culture of personal careerism and bureaucratic self-interest to thrive" among some senior officers.[85] In the words of the Somalia commissioners, this has made the officers prone to "deep moral and legal failings."[86]

One of the key points to emerge from the "Somalia debacle," Oliver maintains, was "the need for an enhanced professional capacity, both within the defence department and the government more generally, to differentiate between valuable opinions" and those with little or no merit. Describing the post-Somalia debate on reform of the CF as "swirling" and "unfocussed", Oliver claims that DND, "desperate for good press," sometimes embraced change that was not necessarily wise. He reminds us that, as a profession, the CF needs the capacity and confidence "to both explain the nature of the evolving profession of arms in a clear-headed, sensible way to fellow Canadians and, where necessary, the courage to defend vigorously professional prerogatives and sound policy against those wolves who, in sheep's clothing, would reform the profession to death."[87] But in the end, like it or not, military leaders in democracies must be prepared to do the bidding of a civilian leadership that often knows little about the profession of arms.[88]

Nevertheless, the officer corps, as the epitome of the military profession, has an essential role to play in the culture of the profession, because officers are responsible for conceptualizing and leading change in a service culture.[89] In democracies, officers, as professionals, have a special responsibility to ensure that the soldiers in their charge conduct themselves in accordance with the rules, values, and customs of a democracy.[90]

From a theoretical point of view, the officer corps has generally been identified as the group that should lead change in military organizations. In the Canadian context, non-commissioned members (NCMs) may also belong to this group of leaders. Unlike in some armed forces, Canada's senior NCMs constitute a group that makes the military a career and they exhibit many of the characteristics of professionals. Bercuson describes the most senior of them in the army, the regimental sergeants major, as "guardians of the regimental memory" since they often serve in one regiment throughout their careers. Because of this permanence, non-commissioned officers (NCOs) are able to ensure that officers' commands are carried out. To maintain this arrangement, Bercuson endorsed a "Victorian" separation between officers and NCOs as necessary, believing it essential in order for good order and discipline to prevail in the army.[91] In Huntington's model, however, NCOs have "neither the intellectual skills nor the professional responsibility of the officer." As practitioners of a trade, not a profession, they are specialists in the application, but not the management, of violence. Huntington's interpretation may be dated, given both the recent advances in NCO education and the increased responsibility thrust on NCOs by decentralized operations such as peace support.[92] Clearly more research is required in this area.

In the organizational culture model, the initial socialization into the profession of arms takes place during basic training. This intense phase of military acculturation is generally believed to be effective in making new recruits feel like members of the organization they have joined. Despite the heavy emphasis placed on socialization in all initial training in the CF, Bercuson cites recent studies which suggest that, congruent with theory on values, attitudes, and beliefs, the socialization process is not as effective as some believe it to be. The extent to which new members of the CF embrace military values seems to be unrelated to the intensity of the socialization process. In addition, the socialization process does not appear to have a major impact on the development of new attitudes and values in junior officers, and while surface behaviours may change, it is doubtful that underlying values are changed. The values a candidate brings to officer training may be far more important in determining the degree to which he or she will embrace the military ethos in initial training.[93] Some support for this viewpoint is found in a recently published study which concluded that military socialization processes had some effect on young American high school graduates, but in most cases the processes only enhanced values and attitudes already held by those who chose to join the military.[94]

The challenge, Bercuson asserts, is for the military to cultivate a military ethos that reflects age-old military virtues *and* today's mainstream values and mores. However, these findings must be viewed with healthy skepticism because his conclusions were based on the assumption that Royal Military College of Canada (RMC) cadets were "totally immersed in a military atmosphere."[95] Anyone who has taught at or attended the college knows that most of the cadets' time is spent in the classroom and the socialization that takes place, after the recruit phase, is often done by civilian professors encouraging students to adopt a profession like engineering. Yet if RMC does not inculcate a military ethos in cadets and if we accept that the real purpose of professional military education is to prepare officers to employ violence in the service of the society, the question is, How is this best accomplished? The Minister's Committee on change in the CF says how this might be achieved:

> A suitable formal education has become as much of a touchstone of military professionalism as charisma, honour, dedication, courage and a "strong right arm." Although the essence of war-fighting is today the same as it was in ancient times ... It is no longer sufficient for

Canadian Forces officers to know which civil or military solutions to apply to problems ... it is necessary that they thoroughly understand the nature of the solutions they aspire to use and to be able to adapt or improvise solutions to suit particular circumstances. To do that, they must learn those basic skills of critical evaluation and analysis that will allow them to tackle any problem that may come along. Put simply, they must acquire the thinking skills that a liberal arts education affords as the basis for whatever technical learning they need also acquire.[96]

To date, however, we have no clear empirical data to tell us if this aim is being accomplished in the CF.

In summary, as the leaders of both the profession of arms and military organizations, officers play what Schein described as the crucial roles of determining, shaping, and reinforcing organizational culture. However, there are other factors that influence the development of military culture besides leaders. These will be discussed next.

3

Influences on Military Culture

Military cultures exist, in part, to bring order to the confusion and ambiguity inherent in war and other military operations.[1] Sociologists have determined that a separate international military culture exists; however, within that culture there are marked differences among the cultures of the armed forces studied. Soeters and Recht have gathered extensive empirical data on military culture. They claim that within the cultures studied there appears to be an evolution from what they call a machine, or bureaucratic and institutional, culture to a professional bureaucratic and occupational culture, and they hypothesize that Canada and Norway, because they have evolved furthest toward the latter model, represent the more modern and even the future pattern for military cultures.[2]

The military organization is one of the oldest and perhaps most peculiar examples of a formal organization that social scientists have studied extensively. Soeters and Recht say that all military organizations share these unique characteristics: the communal character of military life, the heavy emphasis on hierarchy, and military discipline and control. They build on Janowitz's 1977 model of the institution-occupation, as developed by Moskos and Wood in 1988, to hypothesize a "presumed process of development of military academy cultures" from "machine bureaucratic/institutional" to "machine bureaucratic/occupational" to "professional bureaucratic/occupational." They observe that militaries share many of the characteristics of bureaucracies, occupations, and professions found in civil society, but in different proportions. These proportions vary according to the national and organizational cultures affecting each military, but Soeters and Recht argue that the trend is for military organizations to be evolving away from rigid, machine-like cultures toward more flexible, professional cultures. They use the following indicators of professionalization to distinguish between machine and professional characteristics in military organizations: *(a)* orientation toward professional ethical codes, *(b)* leadership based on professional competence, and *(c)* horizontally situated reference groups (i.e., role models coming from innovative and leading colleagues within and outside the military organization as opposed to just those in the military hierarchy). The "machine bureaucratic/institutional" military organization tends to have high levels of power distance and high levels of uncertainty avoidance, whereas the "professional bureaucratic/occupational" military organization tends to have lower power distance and a higher tolerance of risk. Soeters and Recht found that, in general, results for "power distance" and "uncertainty avoidance" in those military academies studied showed a "fair correspondence" with results obtained in studies of civilian organizations in the same countries as the military academies. In other words, "in terms of bureaucratic tendencies virtually every military academy resembles the country it belongs to."[3]

In their research, Soeters and Recht also found that personnel in military organizations are assuming an increasingly "occupational orientation," although this varies among the countries studied. Those individuals with a higher occupational orientation show tendencies to live outside the direct military environment, to strive for market wages, and to acquire civilian professional qualifications that can be used outside the military. Canada and Norway, and to a lesser extent the US and Denmark, show a cultural pattern that is relatively more professional bureaucratic and occupational compared to other countries, and Soeters and Recht observe that the shift in military organizational cultures around the world seems to be in this direction. For this reason they hypothesize that Canada and Norway represent "the more contemporary or even the future form of military life." Soeters and Recht note that their findings have important implications for those involved in leadership roles in multinational or coalition forces in the future, because differences in military organizational culture will lead to differences in doctrine and in reactions to various leadership styles. They caution that leaders in multinational operations should understand that their leadership and managerial styles may not be understood in the same manner by military personnel of different countries, not to mention civilians (e.g., those working for non-governmental organizations – NGOs).[4]

Many factors influence the development of any organizational culture, including military culture. Most discussions of military culture in the current literature have used James Burk's conceptualization of military culture as an entity with four constituent parts: discipline, professional ethos, ceremonial displays and etiquette, and cohesion and esprit de corps.[5] As stated in chapter 1, this analysis encompasses the three elements of discipline, ceremonial displays and etiquette, and cohesion and esprit de corps under the more inclusive topics of professional ethos and the relationship between the armed forces and society because these two overarching factors determine the nature of many lesser factors, including the three identified above. These two overarching factors will be discussed next and their influence on the Canadian and American military cultures will be examined in the sections that follow.

THE RELATIONSHIP BETWEEN ARMED FORCES AND SOCIETY – THEORETICAL APPROACHES

One of the most powerful factors influencing the evolution of military culture is the national culture within which the military culture exists. The interaction between these two cultures helps define the nature of military culture and, in many cases, the cultures of a nation's armed forces can have a reciprocal influence on the development of a national culture. The Canadian forces' feats of arms in the First World War and the Second World War, such as those at Vimy Ridge in 1917 and Normandy in 1944, helped to shape Canada as an independent and modern nation.[6] Other counties are also influenced by their armed forces' actions and culture. For example, for political and cultural reasons, Belgium has decided that its army must be 60 per cent Flemish-speaking and 40 per cent French-speaking. Since the end of conscription in 1994, it has been increasingly difficult to maintain the Flemish-speaking quota in the army, but any attempt to change the balance has been described as threatening the keystone of Belgian society. For the first time in its history, Belgium is considering enrolling foreigners in its army to maintain the Flemish-Walloon balance and to reflect the more multicultural nature of Belgian society.[7] From this example it is clear that the ability of the officer corps to effect change in the organizational culture of its force will always be constrained by certain factors, such as the armed forces' roles and the nature of the society in which the armed forces exist. It is consequently important to understand the nature of relationships between armed forces and societies before discussing the nature of Canadian and American military culture.

The study of the relationships between armed forces and societies is "eclectic and multidisciplinary," and includes such disciplines as anthropology, history, politics, sociology, psychology, and economics.[8] Western armed forces trace their roots back to the ancient Greeks and Romans, and the forces' relationships with their societies have been studied since at least the time of Machiavelli. Although empirical research on this topic is still in its early stages, a number of conceptual frameworks have been advanced to try to explain the relationship between armed forces and their societies. Research has followed several different approaches, including cross-national comparisons and the relationship between armed forces and society within different categories of states.

Edmonds tells us that the relationship between armed forces and society, referred to as civil-military relations in some disciplines, is a relatively new field of study and he advocates a multidisciplinary approach to research because of the multi-faceted nature of the subject. However, this type of approach only began in the mid-1950s. Older works, usually written by historians, focused on decision-making between military and political elites in time of conflict, and little attention was given to the wider issues of the place of armed forces in society or the interaction between armed forces and their societies. Two key works that sparked the modern debate on civil-military relations in the West were Samuel Huntington's 1957 book *The Soldier and the State* and Morris Janowitz's *The Professional Soldier*, published in 1960.

Huntington's *The Soldier and the State* has largely defined the academic debate on military professionalism and civil-military relations.[9] He examined the relationship between American society and the large post–Second World War armed forces in the US in the context of the traditional American belief that large standing armies are a threat to democracy – the reason the architects of the US Constitution prescribed that no national army should be raised except in time of "real and imminent threat." Janowitz used a sociological approach to inquire into whether the US armed forces, having become a permanent and powerful institution of the state after the Second World War, constituted a threat to American society. He concluded that the motives of the officer corps were more narrow and professional than political and inimical to the American Constitution. For others, however, the fear of large standing armed forces is justified.[10] For example, the late Carl Builder, a leading American analyst of the US defence establishment, asserted that the "most powerful institutions in the American national security arena are ... the Army, Navy, and Air Force – not the Department of Defense or Congress or even their commander-in-chief, the president," and that the military has become too independent of civilian control.[11]

Edmonds provides a theoretical framework to examine these issues based on the following assumptions:

a. Some societies, for reasons of ideology, geopolitics, and culture, have displayed a greater propensity to resort to war or violence than others, and the organized use of force and violence is the principal function of the armed forces of society.
b. The very existence of armed forces within a society alters the perceptions of members of that society and, by extension, the nature of the armed forces affects those perceptions.
c. Armed forces help to shape people's perceptions of the threat to that society.
d. Those who serve in the armed forces have "an immense potential economic, political and social influence" on society.
e. We should be aware of the potential self-interest of armed forces and their allies in society (e.g., the military-industrial complex) in maintaining the present international system and defining threats to society. (Edmonds wrote this before the end of the Cold War but the assumption is equally applicable today.)

f. In societies where the political culture is "low" or "minimal" (e.g., the Third World) the armed forces have frequently intervened in the affairs of government.
g. In order to study civil-military relations, there must be a clear differentiation between "what is military in an institutional sense, and the more encompassing civil, social order"; this approach tests the assumption that all armed forces have "dominant characteristics" irrespective of the society they serve.[12]

In 1962, Rappaport postulated that the relationship between armed services and society is a determining influence on the type of society that emerges. Based on this assumption, he proposed three broad types of society: (1) praetorian states, the most prevalent, where the armed services exist to defend those persons in power; (2) the civil and military polity, where, with internal political stability assured, the primary function of the armed forces is defence against external threats (many Western nations fall into this category); and (3) the nation-in-arms, where the dominant function of the armed services is public duty (Israel is the clearest example of this category).[13]

From their work in 1974, Welch and Smith arrived at a general, comprehensive theory of the relationship between armed services and society. The results of their study have been placed in a matrix, which included most of the states of the world, to explain what type of system each state had and to give an indication of how each might alter its position in the matrix. The matrix was based on four variables: (1) the extent of popular participation in decision-making; (2) the strength of civil institutions; (3) the political strength of the armed services; and (4) the degree of overlap between civil and military institutions. This theory has its shortcomings, according to Edmonds, because of the authors' preoccupation with praetorian military regimes, less advanced industrial states, and communist political systems.[14]

THE RELATIONSHIP BETWEEN ARMED FORCES AND SOCIETY – HISTORICAL CONTEXT

The modern debate on the relationship between armed forces and society has its origins in the Renaissance. The Italian writer and political functionary Machiavelli introduced the modern era in the development of political thought, especially as regards the relationship between armed forces and society. He was one of the first to recognize the link between changes in military organization and the revolutionary developments in the social and political sphere in his time. He advocated a citizen conscript army as the basis of a republic in order to minimize the influence of elites and to overcome the unreliability of mercenary bands hired by the state. Machiavelli's idea of a citizen conscript army as the bulwark of a republic still finds favour in many segments of American society today. Adherents to this point of view claim that citizens owe an obligation of military service to the republic in return for the freedoms and other benefits they receive from it. These ideas were developed by Renaissance writers, like Machiavelli, who believed that the classical (Greek and Roman) world was a "perfect" model upon which to build new European states. The Greek city-states and the Roman republic were held up as the epitome of the republican form of government. The martial successes of the Greeks and Romans were used as examples of how the citizen army was superior to any other – however, the eventual collapse of the Greek and Roman Empires was usually overlooked by Renaissance writers.

Machiavelli's fundamental thesis was that military forces must be composed of inhabitants of the state the army is expected to defend because patriotic enthusiasm can only be expected of an army composed of men fighting for their native land. In addition, the defence of the state is not a task that should be assigned to a special, privileged group; rather, it should be the concern of all those living in the same society. Machiavelli went on to assert that because the life of the state depends on the excellence of the army, political institutions must be organized to create favourable preconditions for military organization. Machiavelli's insight into the nature of war and the role of the military establishment in the structure of society is the foundation of his military thought. As the issues he deals with are not limited to a particular historical period, they are still key concepts in the study of society and armed forces.[15]

The era of modern armies began, according to John A. (Jack) English, when a new type of warfare spelled the end of private war by freelance companies of soldiers of fortune. It was ushered in with Charles VII's invasion of Italy in 1494, because for the first time in modern history a large permanent army (of 30,000) was raised based on regular pay from the royal treasury and command by office-holders (*officiers*) appointed by the ruler. However, it was Maurice of Nassau who was the "father of modern military organization." He introduced the concept of "officership," stressing education in military art and science over a reliance on knightly virtues. Gustavus Adolphus carried Maurician-style reforms a quantum leap farther in scale and scope. He built on a national conscript force to create a long-service army of career soldiers paid from a central treasury, led by an educated regular officer corps, and imbued with rigorous discipline. In the eighteenth century, European armies rediscovered, from their Roman models, the importance of good administration to ensure that armies would be regularly paid, fed, and maintained with supplies. This rediscovery provided the basic underpinning of discipline that characterized the operations of European field armies. In turn, good administration formed the foundation for the development of educated regular officers, promotion by merit instead of class, and the officers' selfless service to the state. Good administration also allowed armies to improve the care of their troops, resulting in the improved cohesion, self-confidence, disciplined ruthlessness, and iron will that shattered the warrior concept of battle more than gunpowder did. These developments, not technology, Jack English contends, were the most important military innovations in the early evolution of modern European armies, and they were imposed by the rulers of those societies on their military forces.[16]

The reverse of this process, armed forces influencing the development of society, began in the modern era with the creation of a "nation in arms" during the French Revolution. A contemporary example, the modern state of Israel, illustrates how the armed forces of a nation can play an active role in the development of the state. Ben-Eliezer describes how early Israeli leaders "viewed the army as the central mediating agent that would transform the heterogeneous Jewish population into a nation possessing the will and the ability to fight a war."[17]

Ben-Eliezer tells us that Jewish leaders in Palestine followed the historical precedents of post-revolutionary France, Prussia, and Meiji Japan in using conscript armed forces to create a national feeling that might help win wars and create national cohesion. The aim was for soldiers, after their discharge from the armed forces, to transmit the values they had absorbed in military service to the general society. The French *levée en masse* of 1792 conscripted the entire male population of France and eventually aimed to not only build large armies but also to ensure the moral and material contribution of the home front to the war effort. In Prussia, the nation-building role of the armed forces was reinforced by militarily-oriented youth groups, student associations, the church, and associations of discharged officers. In Meiji Japan (1868–1912), the army used conscription as a school for inculcating the population with nationalist and militarist values. This program was augmented further by having retired officers placed in schools as teachers. Israel's first prime minister and defence minister, David Ben-Gurion, employed methods similar to the Japanese Meiji rulers in forming an army based on a constitution that embraced the concept of the nation-in-arms. He created a broad-based conscript army with militia-like elements that was deeply involved in the creation of the state of Israel. For example, the army was placed in charge of the transit camps where most new immigrants were initially housed. This allowed military personnel to socialize the new immigrants – for example, teaching them Hebrew – in ways that would prepare them to be citizens of the new state of Israel. An extensive system of reserves was also established "not to introduce civilian patterns into the army but to bring the army to the Jewish population."[18]

The outcome of this program in the 1950s was what Ben-Eliezer called "'positive militarism' in which people show readiness, even enthusiasm, to fight." However, this growth of militarism led to an attitude in Israel where "war not only becomes possible; it is considered reasonable and legitimate."[19] This has led the Israeli state to follow the "'way of the gunsight'" where, by establishing a state based on "the cultural militarism of the nation-in-arms and the militaristic policies of the leadership," a militaristic ideology that saw war as inevitable and right evolved.[20]

The aftermath of the Six-Day War of 1967 marked the zenith of the evolution of the nation-in-arms in Israel. From 1967 to 1973, war-hero generals became objects of admiration and emulation in Israeli society. At this time, "Israelis revered military solutions" to the nation's problems, reinforced by the "parachuting" of just-retired senior Israeli Defence Force (IDF) officers into politics, including prime ministers and cabinet ministers with impressive military records. According to Ben-Eliezer, this was a flaw in Israeli society because it helped to dissolve the remaining differences between its military and civil cultures. After the IDF's poor performance during the Yom Kippur War in 1973, there was some criticism of the IDF, but the nation-in-arms model was not criticized; instead it was decided that efforts must be redoubled to prevent a recurrence of the failures during the Yom Kippur War. But Ben-Eliezer points out that, "It took the Lebanon War of 1982, the Intifada, the Palestinian uprising in the territories in the late 1980s and early 1990s to bring about a tangible devaluation of the model of the mobilized society. These events altered the perception of the IDF's character, status, and prestige among Israelis. The sharp decline in the nation-in-arms model was manifested in the politics that separated army from society." Government policies also led to the decline of the nation-in-arms: the size of the regular army was cut in the early 1990s, and by the mid-1990s "about 30 percent of all eighteen-year-old Israeli Jewish males were not doing army service, compared to less than 10 percent in the past." It was also observed that young Israelis were less motivated to do army service. Public criticism of the IDF indicates that the Israeli army is becoming less of an "army-nation," and Ben-Eliezer believes that Israel may be entering a post-militaristic era but that it is still too early to be certain.[21]

In the year 2000, there were reports in the press claiming that Israel's military was "in crisis," because it was at odds with the prime minister (Ehud Barak at the time) and had been badly damaged by radical changes in Israeli society over the past decade. A recent Israeli government report found "serious deficiencies" in the force's combat readiness – training had deteriorated, many armoured fighting vehicles were not ready for combat, and emergency ammunition stocks were depleted. Part of the problem has been attributed to the boom in the Israeli technological industry, because the best graduates go into industry, and "the last thing" ambitious young people want to do is to join the military. This has had a damaging effect on the regular officers and NCOs who form the backbone of any conscript army. There are "ominous signs that the Israeli army is not what it was." According to a recent press report, very low-intensity operations like the riot control operations that have become a routine part of IDF operations require high standards of junior leadership and this is apparently lacking. Another effect of the social changes in Israel is that few of the Israelis who want peace choose the army as a career, and more Israelis than ever before seek to avoid conscription. As a result, the army has moved toward the political right. In the 1960s and 1970s, when Israel fought major wars with its neighbours, the regular servicemen and women were predominantly secular and apolitical. Now there is a distinctly right-wing religious stance in the army, creating a potential for greater violence in any internal security operations against Palestinians. This has added to tension between the army and political leaders. Because of their military background, politicians "assume they know everything and have a much greater tendency to interfere in military decision-making."[22] The Israeli model of a militarized state is an extreme example of civil-military relations in a democratic state. A more moderate model can be found in the US.

THE RELATIONSHIP BETWEEN ARMED FORCES AND SOCIETY – THE UNITED STATES

The relationship between the US armed services and American society has varied during the country's history. The post–Second World War debate on the relationship between armed forces and society started by Huntington in 1957 and Janowitz in 1960 continues today with many studies and scholarly works examining the relationship in some detail. Edmond's 1990 *Armed Services and Society* provides a summary of the key developments in the literature and a theoretical framework for the study of the relationship between armed forces and society. As shown above, the relationship between armed forces and society varies according to the nature of the state. When Americans discuss the state of civil-military relations, they are usually referring to the concept of civilian control – i.e., Does the military do what their civilian superiors want?[23] But Edmonds points out that the very existence of armed forces within a society alters the perceptions of the members of that society. He also notes that even when ostensibly under civilian control, armed forces constitute a major source of power and political influence within society. Besides the raw military power at their command, armed forces can also wield significant influence in such areas as scientific and technological research and development, industrial output, regional development, and communications, all of which is sometimes denoted by the term "military-industrial complex." This explains why in some societies "great anxiety is generated" when armed forces are believed to be acting in secret without accountability.[24]

Central to Huntingdon's search in 1957 for an answer to his question of whether or not American ideals of liberal democracy had been compromised by increases in the size of the country's peacetime armed forces was the concept of professionalism examined in the previous chapter. Military professionalism, according to Huntington, is the key to civilian control over the armed forces. It is far preferable to use the device of professionalism in the armed forces as an objective method of control than to employ the subjective means of maximizing civilian authority over the forces. Huntington acknowledged that in some states he examined, the prevailing ideology was wholly incompatible with Western concepts of professionalism, except in terms of paid experts comprising the military. However, he believed that, with professionalism, the armed services of most Western countries would themselves promote military efficiency while still recognizing the services' subservience to the state. This was, in his view, better than imposing civilian values and directives which might impair the efficiency of the armed services. Huntington's ideas were in tune with the "new conservatism" of post–Second World War America, where the need for a large and efficient standing army was recognized. The concept of professionalism was thought to ensure that the US armed services would embrace both the highest standards of performance and an obligation to serve society. Nevertheless, in 1962 Finer noted that in certain circumstances the armed services of a state may be constitutionally required to intervene in government as a measure of last resort and a matter of professional duty. This illustrated that professionalism alone was not a guarantee of non-involvement in politics. The universality of Huntington's theory of military professionalism has also been challenged because certain ideal conditions, such as a balance between the requirements of the armed forces and the values of society, would have to prevail for the theory to apply in all cases. Janowitz's 1960 study of the post–

Second World War American armed services concluded that while there had been changes in the professional officer corps and the armed services' organizational structure, the American armed services had maintained their professional distinctiveness and integrity. Their professional ethic, he concluded, was adequate for maintaining civilian political supremacy without compromising the services' professional autonomy.[25]

Hillen is one of many American commentators who has been part of a recent debate in the United States on a perceived "gap" between the values and ethos of American society and its armed forces. He describes the main influences on American military culture as functional, legal, and social. The gap between the US armed services and American society, Hillen concludes, varies according to the balance between social and functional imperatives, and he argues that the gap should be maintained because the functional imperative of war fighting requires it.[26] A contrary view is provided by Sarkesian et al., who suggest that, while the military culture must take its combat role into account, unless the military is sensitive to domestic social issues and prepared to change its culture to conform to societal norms, it may lose its legitimacy in the eyes of American society.[27]

As significant changes in the US armed services (e.g., policies affecting the terms of service of women and homosexuals) have been mandated by the government in the past few years, a debate has arisen in the American press and academic literature over the proper relationship between the US armed services and society. One side of the debate contends that the proper "ethos" for the US armed forces should be based on the assumption that "Winning the nation's wars is the military's functional imperative. Indeed, it is the only reason for a liberal society to maintain a military organization."[28] Therefore, the armed forces should maintain a gap in values and ethos between themselves and civil society. The other side of the debate asserts that the armed forces must change with society if they wish to maintain the support of American society and their viability as the military forces of a democratic nation. But personnel changes in the US armed services since the Second World War have affected their relationship to US society and created perceptions of a gap between the military and society. Until the draft was ended in 1973, the Cold War forces of the US were based on a large conscript army that generally reflected the makeup of US society. Most male Americans served in uniform in one capacity or another and in the thirty years after 1942 the US could be said to have many of the characteristics of a nation-in-arms. Military values and ethos were intermingled with societal values and ethos as large numbers of American males of all walks of life returned to civil society after their military service. However, since 1973, in theory, the US armed forces have returned to an "all-volunteer" military. Yet, despite the "all-volunteer" policy of the forces, it has been recognized that they practice an "economic draft" that reflects American class divisions, because "the working class and people of colour predominate" in the ranks of the military. They join the US military for various reasons, but the ranks of the US military are no longer representative of society as a whole.[29] In some ways this reflects the characteristics of Canada's armed forces.

THE RELATIONSHIP BETWEEN ARMED FORCES AND SOCIETY – CANADA

As with our American neighbours, the proper relationship between the armed forces of Canada and civilian society has been a controversial topic in this country. Canada's first defence minister, Sir Georges-Étienne Cartier, proclaimed that Canada's militia would be a key institution in building the new nation.[30] This role has recently been reaffirmed by the Minister of National Defence (MND). Still, for much of Canada's history its armed forces have been marginalized in peacetime and they were the cause of national crises over conscription in the First and Second World Wars. The current debate over the proper relationship between the Canadian Forces and civilian society has its most recent roots in the integration and unification of the CF in the 1960s. The Commission of Inquiry into the CF deployment to Somalia concluded in 1997, however, that many of the issues raised about the relationship between the CF and civilian society over at least the past twenty years had not been satisfactorily resolved.

The purpose of this section is to examine some of the issues in the relationship between the Canadian Forces and civilian society over the past two decades in order to better understand how the relationship between the CF and Canadian society can influence Canadian military culture, a topic which will be discussed in detail later.

The debate over the proper relationship between the CF and Canadian society was reignited twenty years ago by Loomis and Lightburn. They used arguments similar to those seen in the American debate, namely that because combat was the raison d'être of the armed forces of the nation they needed to maintain "an identifiable subculture within Canadian society." Loomis and Lightburn argued that nurturing the primary group was one of the key elements in preserving combat capability, and that the integration of the CF into the mainstream of Canadian society and the maintenance of effective military forces was "an impossible contradiction."[31] Broadbent acknowledged there was a perception that civilian values had been replacing military values in the CF and that Loomis and Lightburn's model of a "secular religion" for the military was appealing. However, Broadbent noted that, in the past, successful armies had used means other than a reliance on traditions to nurture the "cohesiveness essential to the effectiveness of the fighting group." He suggested that the key to successful adaptation to changes in society by the CF lay in being able to "differentiate between 'traditional necessities' and 'necessary traditions.'"[32]

Implicit in Loomis and Lightburn's, and Hillen's, arguments is the notion that to foster cohesion in primary groups, each group must be homogeneous. In other words, women, homosexuals, and perhaps other "outsiders" would disrupt the bonding that is necessary to produce the cohesion required for combat effectiveness in most male groups. This argument was made explicitly by Mackubin Thomas Owens who argued that, based on the model of ancient Greek armies, the US military culture should not be modified to comply with government policies of "multiculturalism, sexual politics and the politics of 'sexual orientation.'"[33] There is not a great deal of empirical evidence to support or refute this point of view; however, the Greeks certainly tolerated, and in some cases encouraged, the participation of homosexuals in their armies. Arthur Ferrill has demonstrated that in the ancient world, depending on the norms of behaviour in a military organization, homosexuality, and by extension other differences, may or may not have detracted from combat effectiveness. The example he gives of the Theban Sacred Band – 300 warriors based on 150 pairs of homosexual lovers, noted for its valour and "one of the finest elite forces in ancient warfare"[34] – certainly calls into question Owens's arguments about excluding homosexuals from the US services because they might be "corroding the very source of military excellence itself."[35]

As the example of homosexuality in the military shows, there are no clear criteria to "differentiate between 'traditional necessities' and 'necessary traditions'" in today's CF. Some would suggest criteria of "utility" or "efficiency," but this has led to what many feel is an over-reliance on business methods to distinguish between what should be kept and what should be discarded in the way the CF operates.[36]

One of the earliest and still one of the best analyses of the rise of a civilian ethos in the CF caused by post-unification "civilianization" was written by Kasurak in 1982. He characterized civilianization in three ways: "a sociological problem" in its broadest sense, "a problem in civil-military relations" at a less general level, and "a question of public administration" at its lowest level.[37] Kasurak concluded that since 1967 the CF "have been civilianized in at least two important aspects: a decline of traditional values in the field forces and the introduction of civilians throughout the headquarters establishment in Ottawa."[38]

In terms of traditional values, he tells us that Gabriel and Savage's 1978 thesis of "crisis in command" – denoting a collective failure in leadership of the officer corps caused by an inflation in numbers, frequent postings aimed at career development, a decline in martial values, the adoption of inappropriate civilian norms and management techniques, and the abandonment of a belief in the military profession as a vocation – has struck a responsive chord in many Canadian officers. While Kasurak says the Canadian "crisis in command" is attributed to "civilianization," he claims that until "the causes of civilianization are understood, policy initiatives designed to correct the situation" may fail.[39]

On the introduction of civilians throughout the headquarters establishment in Ottawa, he argues that "large-scale and long-term social forces are at the root of the problem" of civilianization, and that "the real nature of the crisis lies in the psychological and sociological condition of the combat arms" which have undergone great changes since 1960, apart from those brought on by unification. Kasurak notes that by 1978 the combat personnel (including sea operations personnel) had shrunk to only 20 per cent of total military personnel and the proportion of administrative and technical support troops had increased, bringing with it rank inflation among those troops. Citing Cotton's 1979 study of the CF – "A Canadian Military Ethos" – and other studies of the American, British, German, and Soviet armed forces, Kasurak concluded civilianization was a "product of technology." As technology has affected all aspects of society more profoundly, it has had many effects. They include weakening the military's monopoly on "functionally relevant information" and fragmenting the military profession into specialist subgroups which have become "mutually alienated." This has led to a decrease in internal cohesion in the military profession. The civilianization of Canadian military headquarters, according to Kasurak, had complex roots whose origins can be traced in part to the failure of the traditional organizational structure to accommodate the demands of new technology (e.g., the Avro Arrow project). But another important factor in the civilianization of National Defence Headquarters (NDHQ), he argues, was the cumbersome staff structure and the failures of the headquarters system to consistently give sound advice to the government prior to integration. While Kasurak suggested that an officially promulgated military ethos statement could be useful in preventing the introduction of systems or technology which could adversely affect the effectiveness of the CF in the moral and psychological domains, he acknowledged that such a statement would be unlikely to reverse the basic trends of the declining number of troups in the combat arms of the army and operational personnel in the navy and air force as the nature of modern warfare changes.[40]

Critchley provides another view of "civilianization" in the CF. She claims that in some ways the military has gained more power since unification, because it has had "a much greater influence – on a broader range and at a higher level – over defence decision making than in the past." She asserts that the "good old days" when the military was in charge of defence policy-making never existed and that it is more accurate to say that there has been an evolution in the structure of the CF from 1968 on. Critchley argues that the 1961 Royal Commission on Government Organization (the Glassco Commission) observed that the vast majority of the 50,000 civilians in DND were employed as tradesmen or junior administrators and that almost all senior positions were held by military officers. However, the frequent rotation and early retirement of military officers undermined management continuity according to the commission's report. The report stated that the sole function of civilians in DND should be to assist the three services and to provide continuity in the administration of programs. In 1964 Bill C-90, which integrated the armed forces under a single Chief of the Defence Staff (CDS), also created a new Defence Council consisting of the CDS, Vice Chief of the Defence Staff, and three civilians and in fact retained roughly the same military-civilian ratio as the old Defence Council of four military and five civilians. Therefore, even though integration in 1964 had a dramatic effect on the old tri-service headquarters, the division between the military and civilian parts of DND remained. Unification of the armed services in 1968 still did not produce basic changes in the organization of NDHQ, Critchley tells us. It was the Management Review Group (MRG) – the Pennyfather Commission of 1971 – that concluded that the principal difficulty with the CF carrying out operational tasks was due to "basic management problems within the civilian and military components of the HQ." It found much duplication of effort and lack of unity of purpose among the civilian staff, the military staff, and the Defence Research Board, and it recommended restructuring the department as a single entity in a single headquarters encompassing both military and civilian functions. This occurred in 1972 when the entire department was restructured, integrating military and civilian staffs from top to bottom.[41]

Critchley maintains that defence decisions in DND are made by a hierarchy of senior committees (e.g., the Defence Council, Defence Management Committee, and Program Control Board) which have always had significant military representation. And, in 1980, when the commanders of Mobile, Maritime, and Air Commands were made members of the Defence Council and the Defence Management Committee, for the first time in Canadian history the military formed the clear majority on the committees that decide defence policy. This is why, Critchley concludes, the military now has more influence on defence policy than in the past.[42]

Bland offers a different interpretation of some of these events. He describes civil-military relations in Canada as "floundering and uncertain," and he attributes this state of affairs to "weaknesses long resident in the structure of the defence establishment," especially NDHQ.[43] Bland argues that one of the key problems in Canadian civil-military relations is attributable to the fact that the "defence team" concept, which treats the CF and DND as a single entity, has no basis in law.[44] He advocates returning to the spirit and letter of the National Defence Act (NDA) which separates "responsibilities for policy-making, military command, and defence administration."[45] In his analysis, NDHQ is an "assertive organization that has thwarted the effort of many senior officers and officials to change the nature of defence policy, of command of the CF, and of the administration of national defence." Bland says that if problems in civil-military relations in Canada are to be corrected, then NDHQ must be reformed. However, he believes that reforms can only be effective if lapses in ethics, command, and administration are simultaneously corrected. This may be problematic, according to Bland, because political leaders have regularly "failed in their basic responsibility to supervise the armed forces of Canada."[46]

Bland goes on to argue that Canada's defence has been burdened with "a sense of strategic misdirection and organizational confusion and ineptness," especially since the end of the Cold War in 1989.[47] He attributes this state of affairs to arbitrary decisions made by the Chief of the Defence Staff and deputy minister in 1989 that degraded the CF's capabilities, left senior officers feeling betrayed, and soldiers in the field feeling that they had not been treated fairly. Even though "serious command and control problems were inherent in the 1972 organization of NDHQ," because Cold War commitments were never fully tested, the flawed command and control structure was never fully revealed. After the end of the Cold War, command and control problems were often overcome by good units and their commanders, but the whole system collapsed in Somalia when a deficient system was matched with a poor unit. Bland claims that the "relationship between the command of the CF and political control of the armed forces is so critical that it must be a first order concern of the minister of defence and Parliament"; however, few ministers have grasped the importance of this point.[48]

Bland traces current problems with civil-military relations in Canada back to the formation of NDHQ in 1972, which was based on the report of the Management Review Group. Because the

MRG's objective was to improve "the management of defence," it overlooked the raison d'être of the armed forces – war and conflict. The newly established NDHQ, created by means of a bureaucratic process, became a single entity that encompassed the CF (military) and DND (civilian) parts of Canada's defence establishment. However, this "single entity" idea has no basis in law and, therefore, "it cannot provide for a single operating head for the combined headquarters."[49] Under this arrangement all staff functions of the CF and DND became combined and the notion of the "defence team" was born. While the "unregulated combining of functions and responsibilities within the defence establishment" had beneficial effects, it also created "serious negative effects" at senior levels. War planning and criteria for operational readiness and military advice passed from military staff officers solely responsible to the CDS to groups and individuals under civilians, such as the Assistant Deputy Minister (Policy). The result was that no one knew for sure where orders and directions for the CF were coming from.[50]

Some of these problems, Bland suggests, can be overcome by segregating "the power that has accumulated in NDHQ since 1972." The intent should be to separate and make distinct, but not isolate, responsibilities for policy-making, military command, and defence administration. He suggests that once this segregation is complete "Parliament will regain control of defence policy and accountability for the control and administration of the CF and DND will be unambiguous." To achieve this objective, the spirit and letter of the National Defence Act must be respected as the legal basis for a defence organization which separates the functions of military command and defence administration. Bland also advocates that a parliamentary committee should take an active part in the direction of national defence policy.[51]

Bland goes on to explain that while the NDA's separation of the military and civilian functions of Canada's national defence establishment might seem untidy to some, its purpose is to "solve the four problems of civil-military relations in modern states." These problems are based on the fact that the arrangements of authority and accountability in the act (1) place the CF under the control of civilians elected to Parliament, (2) restrict the use of the CF by the government of the day, (3) provide clear instructions for and an instrument to maintain discipline in the CF, and (4) guard the prerogatives of ministers to decide defence policy and to direct the armed forces. "The NDA also clearly indicates that the government is responsible for the formulation of national policy, the CDS is responsible for the command of the CF, and the deputy minister is responsible for the public administration of the defence department. Ambiguity only arises when politicians, officers or officials permit it by, for instance, confusing shared responsibilities for national defence with collegial responsibility for its various aspects."[52] According to General G. Thériault, a former CDS, the officer corps at times "has great difficulty differentiating between its own institutional interests and aspirations and the real interests of the state, viewing both as coincident when, in fact, they are often very different."[53]

Politicians have displayed a fairly consistent attitude toward the military throughout our history, according to Bland. If there is no threat and if someone else is willing or obliged to defend Canada, then defence expenditures are deemed to be unnecessary. No prime minister would want to make unnecessary expenditures and it follows that no prime minister would want extraneous factors to impose such expenditures on the national budget. Therefore, most governments have seen keeping defence issues out of the public eye as the best policy. It was for this reason that Brooke Claxton, MND from 1946 to 1954, emphatically warned the chiefs of staff that "I am all for silent soldiers as well as sailors," and threatened to remove any officer who "was not content to express his opinions in private." He also worried about overzealous junior staff officers and cautioned the Chiefs of Staff Committee against military planning that sought "ideal solutions" without due regard for "the facts of national life." Every prime minister and most defence ministers, before and since, have expressed similar sentiments at one time or another.[54]

Bland's arguments appear to be valid when examining aspects of the future relationship between the CF and Canadian society as mapped out in "Strategy 2020," which states the following:

> *The Defence mission is to defend Canada and Canadian interests and values while contributing to international peace and security.* [Italics in original]
>
> As a major federal institution, Defence is also expected to: contribute to the achievement of the Government's priorities; comply with

> mandated requirements, such as official languages, environmental protection and employment equity …
>
> Our allies in NORAD and NATO, in turn, want Defence to be a competent partner capable of playing a meaningful role in combined operations; therefore, our armed forces must be inter-operable with our main defence partners in the UN, NATO and coalition operations. This means that Defence must keep pace with new military concepts, doctrine and technological change.[55]

These statements indicate that DND intends to be a lead agency in implementing government social policies while maintaining combat capable forces. It remains to be seen if this is achievable given the resources available. On the other hand, the changing nature of Canadian society including increased ethnic, cultural, and linguistic diversity and the reduction in the traditional recruiting base of the CF indicates that the CF will need to remain closely linked to Canadian society if it wishes to survive as an institution. Whether or not the links can be maintained will in large measure be determined by the ethos of society and the ethos of the military.

ETHOS AND MILITARY CULTURE

Military culture and ethos are closely linked, so much so that they are often used interchangeably in the literature. Whether an ethos defines culture or vice versa has become a "chicken and egg" debate that has yet to be resolved. In this discussion the term *ethos* will therefore be used as it is in each of the sources cited. It is recognized that this is not a completely satisfying approach, but using the terms *culture* and *ethos* when applied to armed forces is another area where more research is required before these terms are clearly understood in a military context.[56]

The sixth edition of the *Concise Oxford Dictionary* defines *ethos* as the "characteristic spirit and beliefs of [a] community, people, system, literary work or person." In the past, as in the present and foreseeable future, the ethos of any military force will, in part, reflect the nature of the society from which it emanates. Therefore, while military forces share certain basic parts of their ethos, societal differences account for variations in ethos among military groups in time and space. A historical approach to this subject shows that certain constant and repeating patterns of military ethos are revealed in a survey of the characteristic spirit of military forces through the ages. These commonalities may be contrasted with parts of the military ethos that are specific to any one military group. The Canadian army accepts that maintaining "the military ethos is critical to the army's effectiveness in war ... If this ethos is absent, poorly developed or allowed to erode, the army is seriously harmed." The Canadian Army's ethos is described as "an all-encompassing military philosophy and moral culture derived from the imperatives of military professionalism, the requirements of the battlefield and the demands war makes on the human character." It is "in part a warrior's code," and it is based on four precepts: duty, integrity, discipline, and honour.[57] In a similar vein, the US Army's ethos is "uniquely informed by the founding values of the republic, including liberty, equality, the dignity of the individual and commitment to unlimited personal liability on behalf of American society."[58] A key part of the link between a military force and its ethos is the officer corps, as the corps is responsible for creating and modifying the organizational culture of the military force as circumstances dictate. However, the ethos of the officer corps itself, as well as those of the military and the nation, will have an impact on the changes the officer corps can effect in an armed force.

The aim of this section is to review the literature on the origins and historical evolution of the warrior or military ethos by surveying some interpretations from the disciplines of history, anthropology, sociology, and psychology. The warrior or military ethos has its origins in the beginnings of civilization and shares some of the controversies that surround other issues from our distant past. The field of military ethos has its own "nature versus nurture" debate based on the perceived importance of the environmental and biological determinants of ethos. Keegan argues most strongly for the influence of culture on the roles, and, therefore the ethos of those who take up arms for their society. O'Connell acknowledges the role of social influences on the military ethos, but he also contends that there is a strong genetic dimension to warlike behaviour among humans. Jack English also recognizes the influence of societies on their military forces, but he focuses more on the role of the modern state and military bureaucracies in "constraining inherent savagery of war."[59]

Keegan's 1993 *A History of Warfare* describes the ethos of the military forces of many different societies. His fundamental assumption is that war has been and always will be limited because human nature determines that it shall be, and he challenges what he calls the Clausewitzian view that war is a rational, potentially unlimited activity as an extension of state policy.

In his review of the literature on aggression, Keegan notes that there are two general beliefs about whether man is violent by nature, which he classifies as "naturalist" and "materialist." Some "naturalists" believe that man is an inherently violent species and that nothing can be done to change this; most "naturalists," however, believe that violent activity is an aberrant trait which can be eliminated from human beings. "Materialists" believe that the human potential for violence only leads to violent action as a result of tangible factors, such as scarcity of resources or poverty, and that violent activity is therefore susceptible to social influence. Keegan's review of the biological research on the question "Why do men fight?" concludes that even though the physical sciences have identified and categorized emotions and responses which are familiar, they do not explain why groups combine to fight others. He therefore turns to anthropology for an explanation.[60]

Some anthropologists have suggested that territoriality and cooperative hunting transmuted individual aggression into group aggression. They believe that this also explains male social leadership, claiming that an aggressive male leadership determined the ethos of all forms of social organization and that women were seen as a biological distraction to the hunting group. This classical anthropological interpretation argues that human society evolved through the stages of band (related by blood), tribe (sharing a common language and culture), chiefdom (being hierarchical and usually theocratic), and finally modern state. Feminist and "progressive educationists" later supplanted this classical anthropological interpretation, according to Keegan, and based their explanations of human social evolution on interpretations of how societies remained stable and self-sustaining. They refused to study war because they believed it to be a perversion of human nature.[61]

Keegan discards this view of warfare and he uses examples of primitive warfare to show that organized warfare was a normal part of the earliest societies. But he contends that the nature of warfare and the warrior ethos were defined differently by each culture. His analysis of the Yanomamo people of the Venezuelan-Brazilian tropical rainforest concludes that most of the violence was based on a competition for women. Even if fighting was endemic in the tribe, much of it was symbolic, bringing death to some but sparing the majority. His interpretation of war among the Maring people of New Guinea, a larger group than the Yanomamo and with superior material goods, noted that conflict escalated from shouting matches through true fighting, to raiding, and finally routing opponents. Curiously, fighting appeared to be clustered around the cycle of pig husbandry. The Maring would not fight without having pigs to sacrifice to their ancestors, and it took ten years to fatten enough surplus pigs to permit fighting. In a sort of circular logic, fighting depended on having fattened pigs, and eating the pigs depended on there being a ritual fight.[62]

Keegan uses the example of the Aztecs, a highly developed civilization, to show that even advanced societies could have a warrior ethos very different from the one we tend to accept as the norm in the West. Human sacrifice was a religious necessity in Aztec society, and warfare was the principal means to acquire sacrificial victims (sometimes thousands were captured in a single battle). Aztec society was intensely hierarchical and Aztec armies were highly organized by an efficient bureaucracy. For them war consisted of pitched battles at close range, but combat was highly ritualized with codes of conduct accepted by both the Aztecs and their adversaries. Great warriors searched for equals or betters to fight on the field of battle; however, there was nothing material about Aztec war making, unlike the Mayans who kept captives as slaves.[63]

These three examples of primitive warfare, among others, are used by Keegan to support his thesis that warfare, and the warrior ethos, is defined by the cultural context of each group of warriors. In each case, society used different methods to regulate the practice of war and the behaviour of its warriors, and in each case a different warrior ethos emerged. A modern parallel to this is the evolution in medieval times of the European laws of war that began to be codified in the sixteenth century.[64]

Robert O'Connell, while acknowledging that aggression is an extremely complex phenomenon, finds different causes of aggression in humans. He notes that weapons in nature (e.g., stingers, claws, body armour) predate humans and that the world of nature is a violent, armed camp; therefore, in utilizing weapons to fight, humans are following long-established precedent. O'Connell distinguishes between natural weapons of prey notable for their unobtrusive and generalized nature, like claws on lions and tigers, and the complexity and diversity found in animal armaments specialized for intraspecific combat, like antlers in elk. Animals in combat with members of their own species follow a set body of rules and their "arms" are matched symmetrically, he notes. The focus is on attaining dominance through a fairly narrow range of aggressive tactics including ceremonial duels to settle individual disputes. O'Connell sees a parallel here in the ritualization of combat and weapons development among humans. He asks if there is a direct causal link between the development and use of weapons and our own physical and mental evolution. He concludes that this is the case because weapons are a kind of vital adaptation normally heavily favoured by natural selection and the virtual universality of arms in human society implies genetic rather than cultural transmission.[65]

However, while weapons may be deeply rooted in human nature, O'Connell acknowledges that true warfare is a rather late cultural adaptation. Even though organized warfare by ants and other social insects was part of nature long before humans appeared, humans transformed war into a dynamic cultural instrument adapting to changing circumstances roughly 7,000 to 9,000 years ago. Some gave up the nomadic life and generated wealth through agriculture. The early agriculturalists then raised armies to protect their wealth from nomadic marauders and armed forces were thus born.[66]

The weapons used by these early armies shaped their ethos, and this is a theme O'Connell develops in some detail. He documents how throughout history fundamental decisions about weapons development and use are primarily reflections of human motives and considerations. The relationship between the weapons and methods of warfare chosen by various societies, according to O'Connell, has been closely linked to the nature of the society itself, and early Greek warfare, like many other aspects of Greek civilization, set the standard for Western warfare.

O'Connell cites the importance of the *Iliad* to the Greeks as the foundation of their religion, a definition of their conception of reality, and as the guide for standards of social behaviour, including combat. In the *Iliad*, both armies are collections of individuals striving for personal glory and a chance to be remembered. The Homeric concept of war was in consonance with the characteristics of intraspecific combat where combat comprised stylized duels between warriors of approximately equal status and whose weaponry was highly symmetrical. The ideal of armoured close combat depicted in the *Iliad* was perpetuated on the battlefields of Europe for the next 2,600 years. As late as the First World War, British public school–educated officers were consciously seeking Homeric glory on what the French called the *champ d'honneur* (the field of honour), based on an ethos formed by their study of Greek classics like the *Iliad*. Heroic styles of warfare developed independently in other cultures, including in India, China, and South East Asia, and remained the dominant form of warfare in these other cultures long after it was subordinated in the West. The heroic style of war gave vent to some basic attitudes and beliefs and some nearly universal themes: fascination with the horse, an emphasis on elaborate body armour, and a general symmetry of arms. The Homeric paradigm is still influential today, for example in our modern concepts of "honourable" behaviour on the battlefield and the belief espoused by some that the Greek warrior ethos is still an appropriate model for today's soldiers. This paradigm is visible in US Army doctrines which both speak of armoured, "dominant maneuver" against similarly armed foes and imply that the pradigm is the most appropriate form of warfare for modern armies.[67] The other, mostly unstated assumption in American beliefs about war is that guerrilla or other non-traditional types of conflict are "dishonourable" and not worthy of "real" armies.

The Greeks, like other societies, developed weapons and tactics suited to their own political, sociological, and psychological paradigms, which in turn defined the Greek military ethos. O'Connell uses the example of a type of fighting that appeared in 675–650 BC based on massed heavy infantry (hoplites) as an example of the influence of social organization, politics, and culture on warfare and the warrior ethos. In this period, the hoplite phalanx depended on the social solidarity of the Greek city-state as it was composed of an army of amateurs and middle-class and upper-middle-class militia, whose participation was defined by their wealth, as they had to furnish their own arms and equipment. But the true significance of hoplite armament and military service was that its possession and use in war were the prime qualification for full participation in the city-state's political life. Warfare as practiced by Greek city-states was highly ritualized. The two warring cities set out exact conditions under which combat would take place, and long range missiles were explicitly forbidden. Even so, combat was costly in lives; it became "a lethal slugfest." Unlike in the civil sphere, where there was a reliance on slaves, in the military sphere, Greek citizens did the fighting and the dying. The Greek practice of legitimizing the political rights of non-aristocratic social orders by military service to the state is the philosophical foundation for the armed forces of many Western nations.[68] This practice was "re-discovered" and transmitted to modern European society during the Renaissance.

At the end of the fifteenth century, for the first time since the fall of the Roman Empire, large, regularly paid, permanent armies appeared on the battlefields of Europe. This spelled the end of private war by freelance companies of soldiers of fortune or mercenaries. Swiss pikemen, who had an egalitarian ethos and fought in a modern version of the Greek phalanx, were the core of some of these new forces, and they were not fundamentally different in organization from the armies of Napoleon 300 years later. Around this time Machiavelli wrote about the new relationship between states and their armies, stressing the close relationship of political and military institutions and the necessity of divorcing politics from medieval moral and personal considerations. The evolution of the mass army with its emphasis on cohesion, Jack English argues, relegated older warrior concepts based on individual fighting prowess "to the dust bin of history." Along with the nascent professionalism of the officers of these new armies, the rise of the nation state exerted a constraining influence upon the inherent savagery of war.[69]

Another new type of fighting profoundly transformed warfare around the end of the seventh century BC. According to Keegan, the rise of horse people from Central Asia, known as the Scythians, was one of the most significant events in military history because it introduced a type of warfare antithetical to the Western Homeric view of war as an honourable contest between roughly equal adversaries. The Scythians were harbingers of a repetitive cycle of raiding and conquest that was to afflict what Keegan describes as the outer edge of civilization (the Middle East, India, China, and Eastern Europe) for 2,000 years. Territoriality, as it was understood in Europe, was foreign to the horse people. For them, war was the process by which they won wealth to sustain an unchanging way of life, and the horse and human ruthlessness together transformed war making for the first time into "a thing in itself." We can thenceforth speak of militarism, Keegan argues, as an aspect of societies in which the mere ability to make war, readily and profitably, became a reason in itself for doing so.[70] The modern analogue can be found in various "rogue" states, such as Iraq, North Korea, and Libya; warlord-led "militias" in the Third World; and some terrorist groups, "liberation armies," and drug cartels.

This same ethos can also be found in some modern Asian armed forces. They are not effective fighting forces, in the Western sense, because a generation or more of military officers, sometimes assuming the guise of warlords, has had self-enrichment as its primary mission. Neither can these organizations be seen as professional military forces in the Western sense, because the principles of self-interest and the principles of self-sacrifice are not compatible, and in Western thinking the business ethos can have a corrosive effect on military organizations. It remains that in Asia the warlord is a businessman who uses military force as a means of enterprise and who combines the military mission with the doctrine of self-enrichment. Warlords arise when the central regime loses credibility and power devolves to regional forces. Since the military is usually the most organized social force, it naturally fills any power vacuum. Some Asian societies, particularly Indonesia and China, are particularly vulnerable to this threat.[71]

The Indonesian case is instructive. During the thirty-two-year rule of President Suharto, there was little distinction between the government and the military. As a former general and one who believed that the army's role in Indonesia's struggle for independence entitled it to special privileges, Suharto appointed military officers as "cabinet ministers, supreme court judges, governors, and directors of state-owned companies." Military officers were involved in every level of government from the highest offices to village administration. Recently, Indonesia's newly elected President Wahid declared that "The military has been politicized, not to serve the state and the people, but to serve the power-holders ... The military has been used by individuals to further their own interests and this must stop." Currently the Indonesian military depends on private ventures to supply about 75 per cent of the defence budget. Interestingly, the smaller, less politically connected Indonesian navy and air force are more "professional" in the Western sense of the word and more committed to reform in the armed forces than the army.[72]

CONCLUSIONS

Military culture is based on not only the nature of a specific armed force but also the society from which it springs. History shows that social organization, politics, and culture have a direct influence on how a society wages war. Conversely, armed forces have an impact on a society's culture, to a greater or lesser degree, depending on its historical experiences.

The relationship between military culture and ethos is complex and as yet unresolved. But differences among the ethos of different armed forces can be explained by a number of factors. First of all, national cultures exert a strong influence on any military force. Next, the relationship between the armed force and the society that supports it determines many facets of military culture. In this section, there were examples of disparities in ethos that exist among Eastern and Western military cultures, based on fundamentally different interpretations of the proper role of the military in society. Even among democracies, Israel and Canada for example, different civil-military relationships have produced quite different armed forces. Furthermore, as Soeters and Recht have demonstrated, there are measurable differences in culture among Western armed forces that arise from differing national cultures and the tension between the vocational and the occupational approach to military service in each nation. These differences in military culture have yet to be investigated in depth, but theories that purport to explain differences among international and/or multicultural organizations, such as those articulated by Pheysey, may prove useful to guide future research.

Another issue that is currently being debated in the military culture literature is the gap that is desirable or permissible between the military and the civilian ethos in a nation. In the US this debate has focused on the effect that the imposition of social policies on the American armed forces may be having on the warrior ethos and the combat effectiveness of those forces. In Canada this debate has focused more on the degree of "civilianization" in the Canadian military, especially among senior officers in higher headquarters, and whether this is good or bad.

While the literature on civil-military relations and military ethos is diverse, the two concepts are closely intertwined and exert important influences on military culture. Civil-military relations and the ethos of both a society and its military provide the crucible in which the values, attitudes, and beliefs of both citizens and soldiers are formed. But the process is different in every society. As we have seen, in a role of true "national service," societies such as Israel have used their armed forces to directly transmit national culture to the society's new members. During the Cold War, those in the US who admired the military virtues hoped that martial values would be imparted to American society by conscripts returning to civil life after their stint in the military. In Canada, since the 1970s there has been a growing acceptance among the public and many in the military that the CF have a role to play in nation-building by showcasing government policies intended to reshape Canadian society.

The Canadian military ethos has taken the form of a statement of espoused values, but there is evidence that these espoused values are not tightly coupled to values-in-use. This is particularly true of the CF's stated desire for military careers to be perceived as a vocation, while the CF's ethos is becoming increasingly occupational. The evidence so far suggests that Pedersen and Sorensen's model of an organization dominated by differentiation, inconsistency, ambiguity, and conflict, instead of Schein's model of a paramount, cohesive culture, more accurately reflects the CF. In any case, this culture may be appropriate for the CF in the future, given the ethnic diversity that will likely be a feature of Canadian armed forces in the twenty-first century, as we shall see later. If cultural diversity becomes the norm for the CF, then Pheysey's explanation of the fundamental differences among cultures around the world in characteristics that are key to military organizations, like control, may be more useful than explanations based on Schein's theories which assume a homogeneous culture and which predominate in the current literature on military culture. These issues will be examined in more detail in the chapters on Canadian military culture and the future of American and Canadian military culture.

From a more immediate perspective, one thing many armed forces share today is the perception voiced in the press and by some members of the military that they are experiencing a crisis of some sort. The next two chapters will examine the nature of these "crises" in first the American and then the Canadian military context.

4

American Military Culture

American military culture at the beginning of the twenty-first century is under significant strain and is nearing a "critical juncture," according to the findings of a recent two-year study by the Center for Strategic and International Studies (CSIS). A number of factors have contributed to this situation, including the US armed services' transition to an all-volunteer force; a change in military demographics reflected in more older and married personnel in uniform than in the conscripted forces of the past; higher expectations of quality of life and job satisfaction from these personnel; unprecedented percentages of women in the US military generally and in non-traditional occupations particularly; force reductions of about one-third in recent years; and an increased pace of operations with overseas deployments increased more than 300 per cent since the fall of the Berlin Wall.[1] Like their CF counterparts, American military personnel feel overworked and underpaid, and believe that they are spending too much time away from their families.[2] US military personnel policy was based on a large conscript force between 1940 and 1973, on a fairly large volunteer force between 1973 and 1991, and since 1991 on a much smaller volunteer force. Yet, despite the "all-volunteer" policy of the US armed forces now in effect, it has been recognized that the forces practice an "economic draft" that reflects American class divisions, because "the working class and people of colour predominate" in the ranks of the military.[3] There also remains what former Navy secretary Richard Danzig has labelled a "psychology of conscription" within the US military today, that still views manpower as a "free good."[4] This attitude may be partially responsible for the human resource crisis that the US military is undergoing today. As the composition of the American military has changed – for example, since the end of the draft the proportion of married personnel in the US military has risen from 36 to 56 per cent – its culture has changed as well. This has resulted in major changes in organizational culture, not all of which may be appreciated by senior officers whose attitudes were shaped in the larger forces of the past.[5]

While many aspects of the American military have received "extensive and continuing analysis" in recent years, no comprehensive review of the "fundamental philosophies, values, and traditions that form the foundation of US military culture" has been undertaken, despite the direct link between military culture and operational effectiveness.[6] Even though no comprehensive study of American military culture exists, a large and growing literature has addressed various facets of this subject. Unfortunately, as Snider has pointed out, much of the debate in the press and academic literature on military culture is largely rhetorical and revolves around social issues in the US, leaving the essence of military culture on its periphery.[7] To facilitate an analysis of the effects of American military culture on the Canadian officer corps and the culture of the CF, this section, therefore, will give an overview of some of the major issues in the literature that reflect the distinct nature of military culture.

Most commentators agree that the chief sources of American military culture are the Declaration of Independence, the Constitution of the United States, certain US and international laws, and more than two hundred years of US military history; however, the debate over the precise nature of American military culture and its relationship with American society has been going on since the formative years of the American republic.[8] Before the Second World War, conventional wisdom was that the American military was deliberately insulated from American society on posts located in remote areas of the US. In addition to physical isolation, the American armed services tended to maintain an intellectual isolation from American society. Huntington and others have observed that the American officer corps has a long tradition of abstaining from participation in the political process, in the belief that the "confidence of the government and the trust of the American people required the armed forces to stand above" partisan politics.[9] This isolation, as noted by Janowitz in 1960 in *The Professional Soldier*, led to a divergence between civil and military culture in the US: "Military ideology has maintained a disapproval of the lack of order and respect for authority which it feels characterizes civilian society ... In the past most professional soldiers even felt that the moral fibre of American manpower was 'degenerating' and might not be able to withstand the rigors of battle."[10] However, US military personnel became more closely integrated with mainstream American culture in the 1950s and 1960s due to the draft which was re-introduced in the Second World War and maintained throughout much of the Cold War. Recently the nature of American military culture has become a prominent issue in debates in both academic and military circles, with numerous articles appearing in journals and other forums, including a project started in 1995 by Harvard's Olin Institute which is exploring issues concerning the role of the American military and the nature of American civil-military relations.[11] The debate over American military culture has many aspects; a few of the contending views are presented next to give the reader a sense of the main arguments in the discussion.

DIFFERING VIEWS OF AMERICAN MILITARY CULTURE

At one extreme of the debate, some US Marine Corps reserve officers claim that American culture is "collapsing": "Starting in the mid-1960's, we have thrown away the values, morals, and standards that define traditional Western culture. In part, this has been driven by cultural radicals, people who hate our Judeo-Christian culture. Dominant in the elite, especially in the universities, the media and the entertainment industries (now the most powerful force in our culture and a source of endless degradation), the cultural radicals have successfully pushed an agenda of moral relativism, militant secularism, and sexual and social 'liberation.' This agenda has slowly codified into a new ideology, usually known as 'multiculturalism' or 'political correctness,' that is in essence Marxism translated from economic into social and cultural terms."[12] These authors go on to argue that if current American military values do not allow US military professionals to realize and act upon the premise that the real enemies of the US are within the American people, then these values need to be changed. In the future, they assert, the US military may need to disobey certain laws, such as restrictions on gun ownership, if the laws threaten "constitutional freedom." They conclude, "The next real war we fight is likely to be on American soil."[13]

Certain writers support these views, and claim that the relationship between American civil and military culture should be based on the relationship that they believe existed between the ancient Greek and Roman societies and their warriors. Some American commentators assert that in the American republic, as in its Greek and Roman predecessors, the right to citizenship is founded on military service. They argue that the success and power of the United States are dependent on its ability to compel its citizens to serve in its armed forces and to "give their lives in defense of the nation."[14] Conservative commentators in the US have emphasized that the "Oath of Allegiance" for new American citizens still contains the obligation for them to "bear arms on behalf of the United States" against "all enemies, foreign and domestic."[15] This attitude has roots in the history of conscription in the US, first seen, in theory, in the Militia Act of 1792, and in practice during the US Civil War and the First and Second World Wars.[16] An early essay in the post-Vietnam debate on the role of the American military in society by Donald Atwell Zoll also addressed this theme, claiming that military service is "the ultimate manifestation of citizenship." He goes on to liken the American military to a reservoir of national values that, even if "neglected by the country," may at some time in the future be drawn upon to reinvigorate an American national culture in "moral disarray." Zoll claimed that by the early 1980s American culture no longer had a pervasive ethical base to provide the social cohesion necessary "to preserve society from the encroachment of militant, volatile, and anti-civilized alien creeds." Blaming "rampant pluralism,"[17] he declared that too many contending belief systems had undermined the "stable core of elemental philosophical agreement" that Americans had once possessed and that the moral consensus among Americans was therefore evaporating. Zoll's explanation of the decline of post-Vietnam American national culture has been echoed by many writers since.[18]

These views have their historical antecedents. Michael Howard points out that before the First World War many people believed that improved standards of living had increased the instincts of self-preservation and diminished the spirit of self-sacrifice among the youth of the industrialized nations of the world. A view common among members of older generations was that the physical powers of the human species, as displayed by younger generations, were diminishing and that the "religious and national enthusiasm of a bygone age [was] lacking." Most European armies attempted to instill what they saw as the proper values into new conscripts, thereby infusing those values into the nation itself as the conscripts returned to civil society after their military service. Some factions of the French Army, led by officers like Ferdinand Foch and in the tradition of Charles-Ardent du Picq, called for a moral crusade by the army to re-establish military virtues in a degenerate civil society.[19] These opinions expressed by military leaders one hundred years ago presage the modern debate about the civil-military gap.

According to Huntington, the most significant issue that may now be affecting the relationship between American society and its armed forces is the growing cultural gap between military elites and civilian elites.[20] This gap is reflected in the following facts: in 1970 there were 320 military veterans in the US House of Representatives but fewer than 130 in 1994; and in 1997, for the first time ever, none of the Secretary of Defense, the National Security Advisor, the Secretary of State, nor any of their deputies had ever been in uniform.[21] The Triangle Institute for Security Studies project on the gap between civilian society and the military indicated that what the institute called the "elite disengagement" from military affairs has been paralleled by what some see as an increased politicization of the American officer corps, with 67 per cent of officers identifying themselves as Republicans and 22 per cent as independents.[22] These figures are particularly disturbing when compared to Janowitz's 1954 survey of Pentagon staff officers, which found that just over 20 per cent of this group identified themselves as conservative.[23] And that conservatism, he found, tended to take a non-partisan form, with military honour requiring the professional soldier to avoid "open party preferences." Janowitz believed that these figures indicated that the military was becoming more representative of society, with a long-term upward trend in the number of officers "willing to deviate from the traditional conservative identification," and he detected a correlation between high rank and intensity of conservative attitudes. Today the available evidence indicates that all these trends have reversed. With the end of the draft, it has been easier for the middle class in general, and liberals in particular, to follow their traditional impulse to turn away from the military. Within the military, the end of the draft also meant the end of its transforming effect on some people from non-military families who would not have otherwise enlisted. Conscripted or spurred by the draft to enrol in the Reserve Officers' Training Corps, these individuals frequently then made the military a career because they found that they actually liked military life.[24] Kohn claims that the current "slide towards partisanship ... signifies a serious erosion of military professionalism" in the American armed services, and that, since Vietnam, many officers have conflated the role of advice with advocacy in both private and public forums.[25]

Langston explains this shift differently and as simply the military's response to ongoing changes in the US national party system. In the past, more officers were Democrats because Democrats were "hawks," but as "hawks," especially those from the South, abandoned the Democratic party, Langston claims, politically active military personnel had nowhere to go except to the Republicans. Langston also offers the explanation that the military appeals to the more conservative and Republican elements of society. This appeal is manifested in the over-representation of Southerners in the US military, as in 1996 the South accounted for only 15.4 per cent of the US population but 31.5 per cent of military personnel.[26]

However, Huntington cautions that the data showing that the military has become more Republican and conservative compared to non-military elites is focused on elites. He doubts that the same contrast would exist if opinions throughout the American public were compared to military views.[27]

Much of the debate in American military journals has focused on the virtues of American military culture. But Peter Maslowski points out that many so-called military virtues are, in fact, antithetical to the characteristic values of American society as espoused by the founders of the American republic. He quotes Samuel Adams to argue that "maxims and rules of the army ... are essentially different from the genius of a free people, and the laws of a free government."[28] While a visiting professor of military history at the US Army Command and General Staff College (CGSC), Fort Leavenworth, in 1986–87, Maslowski claimed that many mid-career officers he met had assimilated military values but had little appreciation of broader societal values. He said that majors attending the CGSC in 1986–87 exhibited an almost unanimous collective contempt toward civilians who actually exemplify national values but do not normally typify military values.[29] The officers he encountered generally espoused loyalty, discipline, obedience, and putting the good of the group ahead of any individual. However, many officers assumed, perhaps unconsciously, that these were the *only* worthy values. "No more profound misconception could pervade the officer corps," according to Maslowski, because within the nation as a whole the values that these officers considered the highest virtues were often at variance with broader social values embodied in the Declaration of Independence and the American Constitution.[30] For example, Thomas Jefferson, the third president of the US (1801–09), regretted the necessity of a standing military force, and he used it for civilian pursuits, including exploration and road building.[31] By the early nineteenth century, Maslowski claims, the characteristic values of American society were well established. He describes that society as capitalistic, unrestrained, and individualistic, where its members pursue happiness through the accumulation of private wealth.[32]

While the founders of the American republic were content to see people pursue happiness, they believed that power was a corrupting influence, and so they diffused it widely in the governmental structure, among the states, the federal government (with its three branches), and the legislative branch (with its two houses). This system of checks and balances resulted in an "atomization of authority." Even then many citizens believed the Constitution did not adequately safeguard personal liberty and they demanded that the Constitution contain a bill of rights as an explicit statement of individual liberties.[33]

From a military perspective, the "atomized" American political system has a number of repercussions. As Korb puts it:

> The president is the commander-in-chief, but the Congress has the power to raise and support armies, and to provide and maintain a Navy, and to

make rules for the governance and regulation of land, sea, and air forces. The federal courts can decide whether the other two branches have allowed military necessity to trample on the constitutional rights of the individual service person without a rational basis. Moreover, this separation of powers and overlapping jurisdictions among the branches, coupled with the openness of the political system, makes it difficult to bring about change in an existing military policy or any other policy for that matter. Thus, the advantage in the American political system, at any given moment, is always with those who favor the status quo or the current policy. In essence, gridlock is the normal state of affairs within the American political system. This diffusion of power allows the military or any group of professional bureaucrats, if they so desire, to play the branches off against each other to resist any change in the current policy. Moreover, since it is the military bureaucracy that must implement the new policy, its members can easily slow down the execution of any policy they oppose. In describing how the Joint Chiefs of Staff tried to undermine his defense decisions, President Eisenhower referred to this tactic as legalized insubordination.[34]

As Maslowski points out, the democratic process is inherently murky, ambiguous, and indecisive because it reconciles competing interests.[35] Despite the potential advantages for fostering personal liberty in the American political system, military people are often frustrated by this lack of clarity in the political decision-making process. Part of the reason for this frustration is that the supposedly "decisive" outcome of the two world wars has created myths that affect how some officers think about defence policies. What Bland refers to as "Proper soldiering," is a "myth centred on the romantic notion that warfare can be conducted according to military ideals, uncluttered by political interference, rules and laws, and civil interests." Some officers carry this myth into the field of strategy, claiming that all important issues will be decided by the force of arms with the unconditional surrender of the adversary the result. Bland argues that those who perpetuate these myths ignore Lord Kitchener's observation that "we make wars as we must, not as we would like to," because it offends their concept of the military's role in society and their "preferred ways of thinking."[36] Perhaps because of these martial modes of thinking in the military, the American people, as Huntington observed, have never been comfortable with professional militaries, theirs or anybody else's: "The Revolutionary War was described as a war of citizen-soldiers against the standing armies and mercenaries of George III. The Civil War was against the West Point–directed armies of the South … German militarism was the principal enemy in World War I … The professionals, in other words, are always on the other side."[37]

This view is epitomized by the actions of one of the greatest soldiers of the United States. George Washington was a citizen first and a soldier second. He rejected personal power when offered the chance to become an American Caesar or Cromwell because he believed that liberty was "the basis for American independence and the national character.[38] This might be the basis for what Langston describes as the American people's increasing skepticism of the military's "right to be different."[39]

THE RELATIONSHIP BETWEEN THE US MILITARY AND AMERICAN SOCIETY

Once the US became a world power, there was more acceptance in American society of the need for large armed forces as an instrument of foreign policy. During the years of the draft, many in American society gradually became convinced that powerful standing military forces were part of the American culture. Much of the subsequent "alienation" between the American public and its military has been attributed to the post-draft professionalization of the military. Under pressure from a perceived civil-military cultural gap, the attraction of a healthy economy, and the stress associated with new gender, race, and ethnic policies, the American military culture has changed since the end of the draft in 1973.[40] The officer corps has also assumed a character that is different from the one it had during the Cold War. Andrew Bacevich, a retired Army colonel who is executive director of the Foreign Policy Institute at Johns Hopkins University's School of Advanced International Studies, observed, "There is a deep-seated suspicion in the U.S. military of society. It is part of the Vietnam hangover–'You guys betrayed us once, and you could do it again,'" This suspicion, he added, "isn't going away[;] it's being transmitted" to a new generation of officers. Richard Kohn supports this view: "I sense an ethos that is different." Officers "talk about themselves as 'we,' separate from society. They see themselves as different, morally and culturally. It isn't the military of the '50's and '60's, which was a large semi-mobilized citizen military establishment, with a lot of younger officers who were there temporarily, and a base of enlisted draftees."[41]

The Vietnam experience was at the heart of the crisis that the US military underwent in the 1970s. Even the US Marine Corps, seen as the epitome of the military ethos today, was "a disaster," according to Ricks. "Drug use was rampant, and discipline ragged." The US Marine Corps also reflected the racial tensions in America at that time as 1,060 violent racial incidents were reported in the Corps in 1970. In addition, it "registered rates of courts-martial, non-judicial punishments, unauthorized absences, and outright desertions unprecedented in its own history, and, in most cases, three to four times those plaguing the U.S. Army. Violence and crime at recruit depots and other installations escalated; in some cases, officers ventured out only in pairs or groups and only in daylight."[42]

Ricks notes a turnaround in the organizational culture in the American military, as exemplified by the US Marines:

> Today the Marines Corps, like the rest of the U.S. military, has drastically reduced its discipline problems. Although there are disagreements over the implications of the changes, I think there is widespread agreement that over the last several decades American society has become more fragmented, more individualistic and arguably less disciplined, with institutions such as church, family and school wielding less influence. These changes put it at odds with the classic military values of unity, self-discipline, sacrifice, and placing the interests of the group over those of the individual. Related to this, and deepening the split, is the fact that while the U.S. military has addressed effectively the two great plagues of American society, drug abuse and racial tension, American society has not. In addition, the U.S. military is doing a better job in other areas where society is faltering, such as education.[43]

This moderate view of American civil-military relations nonetheless reflects the belief of many conservatives in the US that military virtues, if applied to American society, would help solve some of the problems afflicting that society today.

THE US MILITARY TODAY

The viewpoint just presented is somewhat ironic, considering widespread indications of dangerous defects in American military culture today. While studies have found that those in the US armed forces have largely embraced traditional military values and that many agreed that the "function of a military force is armed combat," there appears to be a serious gap between the espoused, traditional values and the actual values-in-use of the US armed services, particularly of the army.[44] Published in early 2000, Breslin's study of US Army organizational culture based on a survey of US Army War College students (lieutenant-colonels and colonels) and "company grade" officers (captains) gives some insight into the army's way of doing things. His data indicate that "micro-management" is "alive and well" in the military and that the "zero defect" culture, despite its drawbacks, is flourishing.[45] Perhaps it is worth recalling that over twenty years ago Gabriel and Savage suggested that the likely outcome of an "up-or-out" career selection system would be a "zero defect" mentality which would result in a risk averse military.[46] More recently, the US Army culture has been described as one that fears failure, with the "'zero defects' mentality …, a mindset fearing horrible consequences for any failure," being widespread.[47] These views were confirmed by the CSIS study whose data was collected at about the same time as Breslin's but based on a much larger (12,500 personnel), and more diverse (all ranks and all services), sample.[48] The effects of these attitudes on organizational culture, according to another survey of over 14,000 soldiers taken in the mid- to late-1990s, was that only about one half of soldiers reported that company-level leaders set a good example for soldiers; over 40 per cent said leaders were more interested in looking good than being good; and about 40 per cent said leaders were more interested in their careers than their soldiers.[49]

Drawing on the theoretical literature in organizational behaviour, especially from Schein, Breslin observed that the behaviour of US Army leaders quickly communicated values and attitudes to subordinates. As with similar surveys, the data cited by Breslin indicated that trust in senior leadership was "surprisingly low," and that units' ethical climates were "under stress."[50] A key factor in this situation appears to be the junior officers' perception that senior leaders are putting their ambition, expressed as a "can do" attitude toward mission accomplishment, ahead of a realistic assessment of whether units were adequately equipped, trained, and manned for missions. According to Breslin, the unwillingness of senior leaders to admit that their units might not be ready for a mission had eroded the trust and confidence of subordinates. The US Army leadership has to resolve these issues, Breslin contends, if its core values are not to be supplanted by careerism. This careerism is reflected in the fact that some officers appear to be spending more time and energy on trying to impress those who evaluate them than on leading their troops. If this is true, then the US Army may not be selecting leaders who reflect the best aspects of its culture and values.[51]

Bell echoed these findings, but he also offered some explanations for this behaviour. He cited a number of sources – including observers from Combat Training Centers and reports published in the Center for Army Lessons Learned – that described "fear of failure" and risk-averse behaviour as common among US Army leaders. One explanation for this situation is that even though the Army leadership manual states that, among other things, leadership must be decentralized, develop trust, and demonstrate risk-taking skills, officers are not formally assessed on these values. The real blame, according to Bell, lies with the current personnel system, which, he claims, undermines trust and is directly responsible for the risk averse atmosphere in the US Army. He explains that the existing Officer Reporting System permits only the senior rater to assign a numerical score to those being assessed. Despite relatively few contacts with the senior rater, subordinates must try to make a good impression on him/her to get favourable scores. This process has parallels with the Vietnam era, when reports and statistical measures, with their obvious drawbacks in reflecting all aspects of operational effectiveness, were used by those remote from the day-to-day activities of front-line soldiers to make important decisions.[52]

These shortcomings in the US Army officer assessment system have taken on greater significance with recent downsizing, where the bottom one-third of the officer corps was purged. This made those who remained more conscious of their professional vulnerability and the army was perceived to be more of an occupation than a career. The downsizing also gave annual "efficiency reports" considerable weight, as one bad report could end a career. Duty with soldiers in the field, once avidly sought, was now avoided because it was seen as riskier than a staff job. Trust became a casualty to career survival in the minds of many officers and the need to obtain patrons became more important than service to country or subordinates. Another factor in this equation was the Goldwater-Nichols Act of 1986, which, while addressing deficiencies in the armed services' ability to conduct joint operations, had the unintended effect of reducing by up to one-half the time majors and captains could spend learning their profession at the tactical level. The net result of these circumstances was that large numbers of officers began to see no professional benefit to engaging in appropriate "risk behaviors" beyond "check the block" assignments.[53]

Despite the implementation of well-focused and well-intended policy goals, many of these policies had results that were unintended and undetected by senior leadership, according to Bell, because the personnel system did not take a comprehensive view of the combined effects of individual policies that were often devised and implemented in isolation. Each policy acted to make officers reluctant to assume risk and each policy compounded the effects of the other. Risk aversion also had what Bell described as a second order effect on the organization's ability to be self-critical, because ideas did not flow freely from individuals who did not trust the organization and who perceived risk-taking as career-damaging. The lack of communication and feedback in the US Army created a gulf between stated (or espoused) values and practiced values (or values-in-use), which grew as individual officers had no way to determine which set of values the army wanted used. Eventually this became irrelevant because at some point the new paradigm became the key to success. Those who adapted to the new paradigm were successful, became the leaders of the army, and rewarded behaviour consistent with the new paradigm, making it clear to most officers where the path to success lay.[54]

The findings of the CSIS study supported Bell's analysis, stating that there may be "a culturally based predisposition to short-term, career-enhancing accomplishments at the expense of long-term institutional needs" in the American officer corps. One outcome of this behaviour was that leaders gained recognition and promotion through short-term evaluations of their accomplishments. However, they did not stay in a position long enough to be held accountable for adverse long-term effects of their initiatives, like decreasing morale or improper resource allocation, if these occurred. Subordinates then saw many of their leaders as "conspicuously self-serving," with little time for mentoring, which was rarely rewarded in any case when it was done. The CSIS study also found that the idealized (or espoused) value of candour remained strong in the US military, but that perceived deviation from that value was a source of discontent among members of the armed services.[55] Recent research based on Mosko's institutional/occupational orientation model confirms this dichotomy, and suggests that the post–Cold War American soldier exhibits characteristics of both types of orientation in what has been called a "pragmatic military professionalism" embracing both institutional and occupational behaviours.[56]

CONCLUSIONS

The morale and readiness of the US armed services are already suffering because of defects in their organizational climate, according to the CSIS study, and their organizational culture may suffer in the longer term. One of the main causes of this situation is that the American military's leadership has not yet adjusted to "the reality that there are insufficient operational resources and personnel to match missions." This may create a "cynical view on the part of service members about the institution's standards and goals and this may erode confidence in institutional leadership." The study goes on to say that the strong local leadership that is "essential for maintaining the vibrant organizational climates necessary for operational effectiveness" is not uniformly in place today. This is attributed to the fact that the "present leader development and promotion systems … are not up to the task of consistently identifying and advancing highly competent leaders." The CSIS study emphasizes that the leader "selection and development systems are at the heart of the matter, and both are intimately tied to underlying military culture." Finally, the authors of the study lament the fact that, despite recent recommendations for change, little institutional momentum exists to force significant change.[57]

Based on all the evidence to date, the CSIS conclusions appear to be overly optimistic about the state of American military culture. As Bell pointed out, some of the institutional factors, such as the essentials of the officer evaluation system, have been in place for over twenty years.[58] Given the importance the CSIS study itself places on leader selection-and-development systems, it seems reasonable to accept that current leaders have adopted a dysfunctional cultural paradigm and are resisting meaningful change to a system they have grown attached to over time.

From a theoretical perspective, the US military today, particularly the army, appears to have a non-adaptive culture characterized by cautious leaders who try to protect their own interests by behaving insularly, politically, and bureaucratically.[59] They tend to value orderly and risk-reducing management processes more highly than leadership initiatives.[60] Much of this behaviour can be attributed to the difference between espoused values and the values-in-use in the US military at this time. As predicted by Schein's theories and modified by Pedersen and Sorensen, new members of the organization have been quickly socialized to these realities of military life, and those who have stayed with the organization and prospered are those who have adopted the value system that worked in the organization – the values-in-use. This indicates that the value systems of the US military and American society are not as divergent as some would have us believe.

One facet of American military culture that is not extensively addressed in the literature is the increasingly multicultural nature of the US armed forces. Race and class differences within the forces have been acknowledged by some commentators, but, generally speaking, service cultures are described in monolithic terms. With 40 per cent of the active US Army drawn from minority groups, more research using multicultural paradigms, such as those espoused by Pheysey, will be required.[61]

According to the Triangle Institute for Security Studies project, concerns about the civil-military gap in the US are justified but should not be exaggerated. The project also concluded that "not all attitude gaps are dangerous, nor are all convergences between the two cultures functional."[62] The implication is that in a democratic state, military culture must accommodate these realities. Nevertheless, American professional officers today have the "intimidating task" of internalizing two sets of values that, in their fundamental aspects, can be contradictory.[63] The discussion here suggests, however, that American officers may have to deal with at least three sets of values: the values of American society, and both the espoused and/or the values-in-use of the American military. The evidence also suggests that the American military may not be the repository of virtue that some claim it to be. Perhaps the values-in-use, and culture, of the American officer corps is much closer to stereotypical American values than many are willing to admit. And if many American military professionals are not actually capitalistic, in the usual sense of the word, then there is evidence that they are at least "unrestrained and individualistic" in the pursuit of their personal career ambitions.

5

Canadian Military Culture

If there is such a thing as a Canadian military culture, it is rooted in the history, traditions, and experiences of Canada's three fighting services – the army, navy, and air force. Very few published studies have examined Canadian military culture, and most of those have focused on the land forces. This chapter will briefly examine the cultural aspects of all three services before attempting to determine if a unique Canadian military culture exists.

THE ROOTS OF CANADIAN MILITARY CULTURE

The roots of Canadian military culture are to be found in the history of the Canadian Army, Canada's senior service, which reflects the unique political, geographic, and demographic nature of the country that spawned it. Prior to Confederation, Canada had small colonial militias for defence, but this changed in 1861 with the start of the American Civil War and the threat of invasion by massive new American armies. The Canadian response was to rely on Britain for guarantees of protection while creating an army rooted in a citizen militia. Basing the defence of the nation on a part-time military force was a natural response at the time because most of Canadian society was contemptuous of full-time soldiers. Our first prime minister, Sir John A. MacDonald, believed that regulars were useful only for hunting, drinking, and chasing women and that they possessed no useful skills. They had taken up soldiering, he believed, because they were good at nothing else. In the late nineteenth and early twentieth centuries, the growth of the Permanent Force (regular army) in Canada was hindered by this contemptuous attitude and the view that soldiering was not a particularly difficult skill to acquire. In contrast to the image of a dissolute regular force, the militia was deemed to consist of "hard-working farmers who were pure of motive and moral" who would fight with "great spirit and daring when the time came to defend home and hearth."[1] For many Canadians, the South African War (1899–1902) was proof that citizen soldiers were superior to regulars in battle. Canadians, mostly "amateur" soldiers, distinguished themselves fighting overseas together in units commanded by Canadian officers, and an overt Canadian military culture began to manifest itself when patriotic songs and emblems like the maple leaf were used to distinguish the Canadian units from other imperial units.[2] Widely reported in the press, the Canadian experience in South Africa – aided by the fact that militia commissions were used as a form of political patronage – ensured that the militia myth continued to dominate Canadian defence-thinking until well into the twentieth century. All this began to change in the Great War. The inefficiencies and incompetence that were part of the peacetime force could not be tolerated in that war, and under fire during the First World War the Canadian Corps became a meritocracy. After the usual peacetime neglect during the interwar years, the Canadian Army in the Second World War once again had to weed out the incompetent under fire. But by 1945, Canadian commanders from battalion to divisional level were second to none among the Allies.[3] This wartime heritage was carried on in Korea where Canada's 25th Brigade was legitimized by wearing not only the "red patch" of the First Canadian Division in the First and the Second World Wars, but also the UN emblem which, according to the *Ottawa Citizen* in 1953, showed it "to have upheld its grand traditions and to have heralded 'a new concept of Canadian nationhood.'"[4]

The Canadian experience in NATO also affected Canadians' perceptions of themselves. They were now seen to be part of an alliance defending the free world against the Soviet menace. The NATO experience also "changed the Canadian officer corps profoundly by professionalizing it," according to Bland. He contends that the militia myth finally died in the Cold War era because the problems of the NATO era were handled "mostly by keeping the professional force employed and out of politics, out of the press, out of sight, and out of the country." Senior military leaders, according to Bland, accepted this state of affairs because "it enhanced the roles professional officers wished to protect and gave them a significant degree of freedom from political oversight." However, he notes that the "end of the cold war also ended this happy coincidence of political and military interests."[5]

Another key influence on Canada's military culture, peacekeeping, began with the United Nations Emergency Force (UNEF) after the Suez crisis in 1956. Forty years later, 100,000 Canadian troops had participated in more than thirty peacekeeping operations (both UN and non-UN). Despite widespread public support for peacekeeping,[6] at first neither the Canadian government nor the military was enthusiastic about it. The military in particular saw peacekeeping as a diversion from "the big show" in Germany with NATO and a drain on scarce resources. This prompted the view in the CF that only soldiers trained for war could be good peacekeepers. Nevertheless, peacekeeping became so integral to the Canadian Army in the public mind that Canadians tended to forget that armies exist to fight wars.[7] While, in terms of numbers, the army has shouldered the biggest peacekeeping burden, the navy has participated in UN missions off the coasts of Somalia, the former Yugoslavia, and Haiti.[8] The little-known story of air force support to the UN started in the 1950s. Between 1950 and 1954, during the Korean conflict, twelve North Star transport aircraft of 426 Squadron carried out 599 missions to the Pacific theatre. The next large airlift was in support of UNEF, and air force support to many UN missions continues to this day.[9]

THE CULTURES OF THE ARMY, NAVY, AND AIR FORCE

Until the late 1960s, the Canadian Army culture was largely a legacy of the two world wars. Its ethos was embodied in an army tried by fire and trained to fight in Europe as part of a larger alliance. Its officers were part of the same Anglo-Saxon elite that dominated the rest of Canadian society, and its ranks were filled by men with little formal education and whose values reflected an older, more structured, less polyglot society. In what Bercuson calls the "old army," very few of the troops were married and most men lived in barracks. They rarely left base and there was little interaction between military personnel and the larger society. For those soldiers who were married, there was little consideration for their families, and a soldier's life, both work and social, centred on his regiment.

The makeup of the "old army" was quite different from Canadian society in ethnic and social composition. Men of British heritage were over-represented, while Francophones and other ethnic groups were under-represented. This was especially true of the officer corps where 73 per cent were of British heritage versus 44 per cent of Canadian society as a whole. The religious background of the officer corps also reflected this divergence from Canadian society as 80 per cent of officers were Protestant, whereas 43 per cent of the other ranks were Roman Catholic, more accurately reflecting the national balance. There was also a geographic imbalance in the backgrounds of those in the "old army." Both Western and Atlantic Canada were over-represented, and Westerners were especially over-represented in the higher ranks comprising only 21.1 per cent of the Canadian population but 31.5 per cent of the "old army's" officers. The "old army" also came mainly from Canada's urban areas, but it was not particularly well educated: the median education for the ranks was less than ten years and only 35 per cent of its officers were university graduates compared with 57 per cent in the US Army.[10] After the Second World War, large scale immigration changed the makeup of Canadian society to the point where now some 30 per cent of Canadians are of neither British nor French origins. In the late 1960s, Canadian society entered one of the most dramatic periods of change in its history. According to Bercuson, post-war prosperity, immigration, education, upward mobility, and the feminist revolution changed Canada forever; it was therefore inevitable and proper that the Canadian Army change with society.[11]

Prior to the Second World War, Canada's navy, unlike its army, had not participated in any nation-defining historical acts, and the leadership of the Royal Canadian Navy (RCN) saw the proper professional focus of the navy as a blue water force prepared to fight in distant waters alongside the Royal Navy (RN) in a major conflict.[12] This is not surprising considering that in 1922 the navy consisted of 450 personnel borrowed from the RN and only about 50 Canadians. Even though by 1927 those numbers had reversed and there were 460 Canadians in our navy serving with 40 RN personnel, the Canadian Navy remained "utterly dependent on the Royal Navy both for legitimacy and for formal training." However, the gulf that had grown between the RCN and the nation prior to 1939 was diminished considerably in the Second World War.[13] It was the "trench warfare of the seas" during the Battle of the Atlantic (1939–45) that provided the "self-defining mythology and lore surrounding the Canadian navy" from that point on. Canada's navy came of age in the Second World War and its identity was deliberately created by the navy and other government departments during that war. This change of identity was possible because the character of the navy changed from that of a tiny Anglophile regular force into the "youthful culture" of the Canadian naval reservists who formed the major component of the wartime RCN.[14] By 1945, with more than 170 ocean-going ships, Canada had the third largest navy and the fourth largest merchant marine in the world.[15] Just as important from a military culture point of view, the Battle of the Atlantic was the navy's Vimy Ridge, where the navy was deemed to have embodied all that was best about Canada and was "'a revelation of the latent power of the nation.'"[16]

The wartime transformation of the RCN's culture had important ramifications for the post-war force, because what a navy can do is largely based on its "traditions, values, and behaviour," what Crickard calls the "strategic culture," of its officer corps. Since at least the Second World War, the "operational ethic" that has permeated the Canadian, as well as the British and American navies, has been the cultivation of a fighting spirit, initiative, and a preference for offensive action. Perhaps more so than armies or air forces, navies have clung to tradition, and this propensity, combined with the "decades-long" lives of ships, has made their organizational cultures more resistant to change than the other services.[17] However, the beginning of the Cold War thrust major change upon the RCN. For the first time in its history, Canada committed itself to a fairly large standing navy, with a fleet of large and powerful new ships to be manned by a professional force planned to be expanded from about 2,500 to 10,000 men. In the immediate post-war years, the RCN started its transition from the British to the American way of doing things, so that by the Korean War, according to Milner, the RCN was "perhaps the only navy in the world capable of working effectively and easily alongside the USN [United States Navy]." Despite some retrenchment under pro-British chiefs of naval staff, the RCN continued its "Americanization" in the 1950s and 1960s. The one thing that saved the RCN, and later the Canadian Navy, from becoming as imitative of the US Navy as it had been of the RN was its 1947 decision to adopt anti-submarine warfare as its raison d'être. Milner describes this as "the most important event in Canadian naval history" because it marked the acceptance of a role that would define the nature of this country's navy. This role fit naturally because in the last two years of the Second World War the protection of the North Atlantic convoy routes from German U-boats had "fallen almost exclusively to Canadian ships." The other manifestation of a new Canadian culture in the RCN was the decision to build a uniquely Canadian-designed and -constructed fleet. By the early 1950s, with the adoption of a primarily anti-submarine role, plans to build distinctly Canadian warships, to adopt North American (as opposed to British) living standards on board ship, the re-introduction of the maple leaf on ships' funnels and the "Canada" flash on uniforms, and the replacement of Trafalgar Day with Battle of the Atlantic Sunday as the RCN's new "feast day," a new Canadian ethos was being developed in the RCN.[18]

This new ethos did not, however, include all parts of Canadian society. Unlike the army, with its francophone regiments, the RCN was almost entirely anglophone, since English was the international language at sea. In 1951, only 2.2 per cent of the officers and 11 per cent of the other ranks were francophone, and 80 per cent of francophones failed culturally-biased RCN entrance exams compared to 52 per cent of other applicants. After the passage of the Official Languages Act in 1969, the navy took some steps to include Québécois among its ranks. It established its first French Language Unit, HMCS Ottawa, and gradually made the service more welcoming to francophones by moving Naval Reserve Headquarters to Quebec City in 1983. This last initiative gave French-speaking personnel a culturally compatible shore billet to be posted to when they were not at sea. By the mid-1980s, despite shortcomings in the bilingual programs, speaking French in the navy had ceased to be an issue.[19]

Today's navy, according to Hadley, "projects itself largely as an aggressive 'militaristic' force," which accounts for "its frequent lack of public support." Having lost its traditional role since the end of the Cold War, it is searching for a new identity by working with other government departments, in such "non-traditional roles" as fishery and sovereignty patrols, and constabulary and diplomatic duties, "seemingly unaware that these tasks were the distinctly Canadian sources from which Canada's naval force had sprung."[20] Nevertheless, the navy's domestic roles in preserving Canadian sovereignty, such as in the "Cod Wars," has maintained the navy's relevance in the public's eye.[21]

The air force, unlike the navy, earned an enviable reputation in the First World War based on the exploits of fighter aces like Billy Bishop and Raymond Collishaw. They were among the 127 Canadian aces in the imperial flying services who together accounted for a staggering 1,500 victories in that war.[12] In fact the top ten Canadian aces accounted for 462 enemy aircraft, a significant portion of the British Empire's total.[23] By accounting for this many kills, the Canadian flyers established a reputation for their country out of all proportion to the small number of them in the British air services. Yet Canada had no operational air force of its own overseas during the First World War, but served as a recruiting ground for the British flying services: the Royal Flying Corps (RFC), the Royal Naval Air Service, and, from 1918, the Royal Air Force (RAF). However, Canadians made a substantial contribution to the Royal Air Force, as by the end of the war about 25 per cent of all RAF flying personnel and perhaps 40 per cent of RAF pilots on the Western Front were Canadian.[24] Less well-known than the exploits of its aces is the fact that Canada – through the RFC (later RAF) Canada – was a world leader in aircrew training in the First World War. By sending 200 pilots per month to Britain, a dominion with less than 10 per cent of the Empire's population[25] produced at least 20 per cent of the aircrew reinforcement needs of the British Empire, and by November 1918, two-thirds of the staff and 70 per cent of the flying positions of the RAF Canada were filled by Canadians.[26] Canadian expertise in aircrew training was also recognized by its closest neighbour. As late as April 1917 (the month the US entered the First World War), there were only 52 trained flyers in the Aviation Section of the US Army Signal Corps; by war's end there were over 16,000 flyers in the United States Army Air Corps.[27] The American expansion was given a running start by the RFC Canada when it gave briefings and instructional material to those in charge of starting a large scale American flying training program. Ten days after their visit to RFC Canada facilities, American officials began their own program using many of the methods and materials borrowed from Canada.[28] As the war drew to a close, two Canadian air services were created. At home, a small Royal Canadian Naval Air Service (only created in September 1918) conducted maritime patrols, and a two-squadron Canadian Air Force was established in England in the last few months of the war. But both disappeared with the coming of peace.

Between 1920 and 1924, the air force made the transition from "a small permanent military service," whose pilots gradually lost most of their military skills, to a group of "bush pilots in uniform."[29] When the Royal Canadian Air Force (RCAF) came into existence on 1 April 1924, it consisted of 66 officers and 194 other ranks, but it did not have the status of an independent military service, as its headquarters was a directorate within Militia Headquarters. The RCAF was involved mainly in what it called civil-government air operations: exploration of the north, charting air routes for land and seaplanes and establishing bases for them, delivering the mail, and forestry patrols. All these tasks were looked upon with approval by a public which was not interested in spending money on defence. While the RCAF sent a small number of officers annually to Britain to take advanced courses with the RAF, unlike the navy, Canada's small air force conducted most of its officer training at home. In 1938, with the approach of war, the air force finally won its independence from the army with the appointment of the first Chief of the Air Staff.

During the Second World War, the RCAF expanded to over one hundred times its peacetime strength, from 1,150 all ranks in 1938 to a wartime peak of 206,350 all ranks at the end of 1943.[30] Once again, Canada excelled in the aircrew training role as the Canadian-based portion of the British Commonwealth Air Training Plan furnished 44 per cent of the 340,000 Commonwealth aircrew trained between 1939 and 1945.[31] Like its sister services, by fielding the fourth largest air force in the world, the RCAF made an important contribution to the Allied war effort.[32] More than was the case with the other two Canadian services, however, as a matter of government policy large numbers of Canadian airmen were sent to serve with British forces – of the almost 50,000 members of the RCAF who went overseas, about 60 per cent served with the RAF.[33]

Immediately after the Second World War, the RCAF was cut back drastically and only five of the eight authorized squadrons found their way onto the regular order of battle between 1945 and 1950. With the coming of the Cold War, the RCAF expanded quickly, and by 1955 the RCAF had reached a post-war peak of almost 3,290 aircraft in forty-one squadrons (twenty-nine regular and twelve auxiliary) with 54,000 men and women on strength.[34] Throughout the Cold War, Canada's air force worked closely with the US Air Force, particularly in the air defence of North America in NORAD and with American air forces overseas in NATO. This led to the purchase of almost exclusively American aircraft types and the adoption of American air doctrine in most roles.

Very little research has been done on the cultural aspects of Canada's air force; however, a few generalizations can be made from the limited material available. Before the Second World War, the RCAF imitated its British counterpart in doctrine, ranks, and uniforms. By the Second World War, the "Canadianization" of overseas squadrons demanded by the public resulted in a gradual shift toward a more Canadian character in the RCAF overseas. At home, the British Commonwealth Air Training Plan not only perpetuated a Canadian way of doing things among the majority of the RCAF who remained on this side of the Atlantic, but it also exposed many British aircrew trainees to a Canadian culture very different from the culture they had come from in the United Kingdom. With the advent of the Cold War and its close association with the US Air Force in both NORAD and NATO, the RCAF (and later the Canadian Air Force) came under the strong cultural influence of its neighbour to the south.[35] As we shall see, the Canadian Air Force has moved its culture closer to its American cousin's than have the other two Canadian services to their American analogues.

A "CANADIAN FORCES CULTURE"

The appearance of what could be termed a Canadian Forces culture, as opposed to three separate service cultures, occurred when the three services were forcibly merged in the 1960s. Some integration took place in the late 1940s and 1950s when the MND, Brooke Claxton, combined the armed forces' medical, dental, legal, and chaplain services, as well as some clerical support. Key headquarters staff functions, such as operations, procurement, and personnel, were also grouped together regardless of service affiliation. Eventually some two hundred inter-service co-ordinating committees were established to try to bring the operating procedures of the services into accord.[36] Bercuson dates the beginning of the end of the "old army" with the Glassco Royal Commission in 1963, which was struck to recommend ways to correct overlap and inefficiency in the armed services.[37] This inquiry was prompted chiefly by the declining per centage of funds to replace equipment in the service budgets. In 1954, 43 per cent of the annual defence budget was spent on equipment; however, by 1963 the figure was 13 per cent, and it was projected that by 1965–66 there would be no money available for equipment purchases. But the real changes came under Paul Hellyer, MND from 1963 to 1967, whose own wartime experience as surplus aircrew transferred to the army – where he discovered drill, medical standards, and much else were not the same as in the air force – motivated many of the changes.[38] Beginning in 1964, reforms such as abolishing the three service chiefs and replacing them with a single Chief of the Defence Staff (CDS) were implemented, and Hellyer's reforms culminated in 1968 with the unification of the three services into the CF and wearing a single style of green uniform.

One uniform and one command structure did not, however, create a single military culture in Canada, and in the mid-1980s distinctive service uniforms were restored, reflecting the continued existence of three service cultures within the CF. But unification did bring cultural change to the officer corps of the CF. With administrative efficiency and bureaucratic control as the main aims of unification, civilian bureaucrats were brought into the military decision-making process. This confused the chain of command and "placed administrative acumen above military insight on the list of qualities required of CF officers." This led to what Bercuson calls the rise among senior and middle-rank officers of the "military technocrats" who, by espousing civilian and bureaucratic values which conflicted with traditional military values, became confused about their proper role in the defence hierarchy.[39]

Other changes followed the infusion of civilian values into DND. As part of the drive for efficiency, many smaller units were moved to new, large bases, and increasingly, military personnel lived off base, "on the economy." This had the double effect of junior leaders losing the close contact they previously had maintained with their men when they lived in barracks and of bringing service people into closer contact with civilian society. In addition, the majority of military personnel now had a spouse and often a family. These trends were also visible in the British and American armies, and were seen by these armies as undermining their military ethos. [40]

THE CANADIAN MILITARY ETHOS

A "crisis" of military ethos accompanied the rapid change in both society and the military in the 1960s and 1970s in Canada, as new roles and missions, structural re-organization, downsizing, and budget cuts took their toll on the old military ethos.[41] The CF addressed this problem in a number of ways: a series of reports were written by those inside and outside the CF; a debate appeared in the Canadian military literature; and the CDS instituted measures to address the "crisis," including the circulation of a draft CF ethos statement in 1981 and the commissioning of an "Officer Corps Study" in 1987.[42] These initiatives culminated in the CF Ethos Statement promulgated in 1997, which was to be "integrated into all recruiting, training, professional development and performance assessment activities at all levels."[43] Given the importance of the ethos of an organization to the organization's culture, this section will examine the evolution of the Canadian military ethos from its origins through the upheavals that started in the 1960s. The goal is to see how these changes have affected Canadian military culture.

There has been a great deal of speculation but relatively little research on the links between Canada's past and its present military ethos.[44] Preston summarizes some of the main assumptions that have been repeated in the thirty years since his essay "The Profession of Arms in Postwar Canada" was published. Referring to the Canadian Militia tradition, begun in New France, Preston contends that the militia has outshone the regimented regulars in both the defence of Canada and in service overseas.

This has its echoes today when one considers that up to 30 per cent of some CF missions overseas have been composed of reservists. Most historians today refer to this as "the militia myth" because a careful study of the classic case claimed as the example of the superiority of the militia over the regulars, the War of 1812, shows that it was the small British regular forces who were the backbone of the defence of Canada. It was actually their skill and discipline that anchored the irregular forces and successfully defended the nation from invasion. The case of New France is somewhat ambivalent in its support of the militia myth. Despite the tremendous contribution made by the habitants to the defence of the colony, by the end of the *ancien régime* during the Seven Years War (1756–63), New France had become a society in arms. While males sixteen to sixty years of age had always been enrolled in the parish militia, by 1757 as many as one-quarter of the male population was on active service in summer. This ruined the economy and contributed to New France's downfall. On the other hand, the determined British effort to conquer New France compelled authorities to call out the militia and to depend increasingly on regular troops from France.[45] The Canadian experience in the First and Second World Wars does not fully support the militia myth either, as it was the transformation of militia units into professional forces through long training and operations that produced the Canadian Army whose reputation shone in both world wars. Preston points out that, in addition to its wartime experience, the militia in Canada has had a long history of maintaining civil order during disturbances caused by riots and strikes, especially from shortly after Confederation until the 1930s. Through its existence, the militia also kept alive the concept of a potential Canadian national military effort and became the foundation for this effort in the First World War. This is still a contentious issue today: efforts to combine militia units or to relegate them to support roles within the CF are being fiercely opposed by the militia lobby, using "the militia myth" as one of their key arguments.[46]

A seminal contribution to the debate over a Canadian military ethos was made by Lieutenant-Colonel C.A. Cotton in a number of writings beginning in the late 1970s. Cotton claimed that the essential characteristic of the Canadian military ethos is the voluntary nature of military service in this country. He noted that the 1980 "Vance Report" had asserted that the CF were, as an institution, "confronting a 'crisis of its military ethos,'" and he set out to examine the issue and to recommend solutions to resolve the "crisis." Cotton claimed that his 1979 report "Military Attitudes and Values of the Army in Canada" had been misinterpreted by some, but that its real effect had been to push "the reader to 'rediscover' the historical truth that the spiritual dimensions of military systems are more important than the physical." Cotton divided the military ethos into two components: the institutional and the individual. He contended that the individual members of the CF needed a written "short ethical code about how members of the military ought to behave and about what their basic beliefs should be." He advocated a military ethos for the CF that was "a philosophical statement of what is valued and desired, of what 'ought to be,' rather than what 'is.'" Many of Cotton's suggestions were incorporated into the current "CF Ethos Statement."[47]

Cotton's work has had a significant impact on perceptions of the commitment, professionalism, and ethos of members of the CF, particularly in the army. However, Flemming concludes that based on a factor-analysis test of Cotton's data the latter's findings did not accurately depict the attitudes of Mobile Command (army) personnel. Flemming asserts that while members of the Canadian Army believed in the importance of a traditional ethos of sacrifice and of unlimited liability to duty regardless of the consequences, they may have had significant reservations about the actual costs of the sacrificial ethos in terms of individual autonomy. In short, army personnel supported the maintenance of a traditional military ethos, but a substantial minority tended to view the demands made upon them as too great. This theme of perceived unreasonable demands by the CF on its personnel in the field seems to be a recurring theme, given that the data from Cotton's work in the 1970s is reflected again in the testimony of soldiers before the Board of Inquiry–Croatia, showing that twenty years later these same attitudes persist.[48]

Whatever the criticism of his data manipulation may imply, Cotton's work had a significant effect on the conceptual aspects of the debate on military ethos in Canada. He used the word *ethos* to indicate "what 'ought to be,' rather than what 'is.'"[49] Using this definition, perhaps the current CF Ethos Statement should be seen as an ideal or desired ethos to distinguish it from the ethos that may actually exist in the CF. Testimony given to the Somalia Inquiry and the Board of Inquiry–Croatia indicates that there is still a significant difference between the actual and ideal CF ethos; it is therefore essential to distinguish between the two. There has been a long debate about whether the CF need a written ethos statement or not. The decision to publish one indicates that authorities believe that an explicit ethos statement is required in order to avoid misinterpretation or corruption of the implicit ethos by subcultures in the CF, as occurred in the Canadian Airborne Regiment in Somalia. The current CF ethos statement appears to embody the principles articulated by Cotton; however, it is an ideal that may never be fully internalized by all CF members.

The "Officer Corps Study" was another attempt to come to grips with the "crisis" in the CF's military ethos. Chapter 4 of the study focuses on the views of CF officers, based on interviews and discussion groups conducted mostly between 1987 and 1989. Using this methodology, a snapshot of CF officers' concerns at this time was captured. Issues such as "service before self," "unlimited liability," commitment, integrity, ethical behaviour, and bureaucratic control were all raised as problems. However, without any historical or other empirical studies to put these perceived problems in context, it is difficult to know if they were transitory or systemic, or whether these problems have any historical background in the CF or the armed services of our allies. Major Lancaster's paper (annex D to the "Officer Corps Study") asserts that "a logically sound and rationally compelling ethos is fundamental to any kind of ethical behaviour," and his analysis of the CF ethos focuses on the views presented in interviews and discussion groups. Interestingly, the views of those consulted appear to mirror findings reported in 1949 by Mainguy, in 1972 by Belzile, and others (summarized at appendix 1 to annex E of the "Officer Corps Study"), and those of the recent 1999 Board of Inquiry–Croatia report. The "Historical Perspective of the CF Officer Corps," at annex E of the "Officer Corps Study," is a useful outline of the development of the corps, but its short length precludes any comprehensive analysis of the factors that shape a military ethos. For example, do these views reflect opinions reported in the past? What are the similarities and differences among these views? Are differences caused by changes in society, culture, or the organization of the armed forces?[50]

Admittedly, the "Officer Corps Study" was supposed to be only the first phase of a four-phase process: phase two of the process was to be "Development of policy proposals"; phase three, "Development of implementation plans"; and phase four, "Implementation of plans."[51] But the process itself was fatally flawed. Without a thorough analysis of all the data and a comprehensive historical assessment of the Canadian military ethos, it is highly unlikely that any useful policies could have been developed using this process.

If the Canadian military ethos was in crisis during 1960–80, some feel the crisis has not yet abated. The murder of Shidane Arone in Somalia in 1993 and other incidents, including the misuse of public funds by senior officers and unacceptable conduct by members of the CF on overseas operations in the 1990s, has led some to conclude that the CF are still "undergoing a serious erosion of military ethos." Robert Near claims that the root causes of the CF's recent difficulties are not fully recognized or understood by higher headquarters. The "checklist" approach to implementing the recent reports' recommendations reflects a lack of any overall strategy, guiding philosophy, or priorities in the approach. In addition, the business management philosophies used in the CF, Near argues, have left senior leaders "consumed with fiscal bottom lines" while neglecting the basic truths that military forces are not limited liability corporations to be constantly restructured, but "living social entities" with cultures that require "care and nurturing." This is also reflected in the CF's Officer Professional Development system which places ethos, as one of seven core themes, on the same plane as management and technology. According to Near, this shows that the CF "still has a rather incomplete and immature understanding of what military ethos actually is and what function it fulfills in a military organization."[52]

Bland offers another way of describing the Canadian officer's ethos by putting it in terms of RMC's motto "Truth, duty, and valour," and by reminding us that it is not perfection that is important, but the promise to live by the motto.[53] Despite the diversity of these views on the CF's ethos, it is clear that this ethos is noticeably different from that of the CF's closest ally.

STUDIES IN CANADIAN MILITARY CULTURE

Unlike the situation with our neighbours to the south, not much research on military culture has been published in Canada. However, the studies summarized below are representative of the state of research in Canadian military culture to date and give us an idea of current Canadian military culture and those areas in which more research might be conducted.

In geographical terms, according to Desmond Morton, Canada's vast size has made it a "country that cannot be defended and can hardly be attacked."[54] Geography has also made the US a major influence on all aspects of Canadian life, although historical experience has given Canada strong European links that some believe can be balanced against American influence to maintain Canada's survival as an independent nation.[55] Another consequence of historical experience has been Canada's "imperative sense of compromise and negotiation in all matters affecting her sovereign political power."[56] This and Canada's long tradition of "nonviolent anti-colonialism," lack of imperial ambitions, and technical expertise has made Canadian military forces ideal for peacekeeping and other similar UN operations.[57] It has been suggested that the peacekeeping role is particularly attractive to Canadians because of the symbiotic relationship that exists between Canadian governments and their armed forces. For their part, since the Second World War, Canadian governments have maintained armed forces to gain influence and persuade friends around the world, and "a century's experience also taught Canada's military leaders that alliance commitments" were almost the only argument that could extract resources from Canadian governments. Canada has armed forces, in part, because policymakers have found them useful for achieving such goals as the recognition of Canada as a middle power, not to mention their role in sharing the North American defence burden with the US.[58] Another reason Canadian armed forces exist is that they have been viewed by some as making an important contribution to the Canadian identity.[59]

Since unification, the CF have gradually adopted most of the norms of Canadian society and have even claimed a "critical role in defending Canadian values: democracy, rule of law, individual rights and freedoms ... peace order and good Government ...

[and] sustainable economic well being."[60] From official bilingualism to the acceptance of gays and lesbians in the military, the CF have often been on the leading edge of change in Canadian society. One interpretation of this phenomenon is that it "reflects a deeper part of the Canadian social and cultural tradition" that is also present in the military.[61] Another point of view is that Canada's military culture has been "demilitarized" by successive governments who have used the CF as a testbed for various social experiments.[62] A third perspective is provided by the Canadian political scientist Albert Legault, who asserts that "a profound gap clearly exists between society and the Armed Forces," especially in Quebec, and that the personnel of the CF are not "representative of Canadian multiculturalism."[63] Whatever point of view one subscribes to, the CF have the potential for a unique ethos and culture based on their parent society .

Donna Winslow is one of the few academics studying the organizational culture of the Canadian Army. She takes the perspective of a cultural anthropologist in examining the breakdown in discipline in two Canadian peace operations – Somalia, and Bacovici in the former Yugoslavia. She concludes that the small group cohesion that is essential to combat effectiveness was counter-productive, in the cases studied, to achieving the mission. Winslow notes that each regiment in the Canadian Army has its own culture which has "depth, duration and collective meaning." This even affects how regiments interpret and solve problems.[64] The aim of the regimental system is to orient primary group bonds into "organizationally approved channels"; however, in the examples Winslow studied, the regimental system contributed to a breakdown in discipline. She found that the regimental system "has itself become a focus of such strong loyalties that it can also impede the good functioning of the overall organization," and that even though the Canadian military ethos prescribes self-discipline and ethical behaviour those values were not universally present in Somalia and Bacovici.[65]

As a cultural anthropologist, Winslow takes an approach that is more descriptive than theoretical. She looks at elements of military culture (the core values concerning cohesion, loyalty, and primary group bonding) as a dependent variable shaped by the Canadian policy of maintaining a combat force. She has also looked at these core values as an independent variable shaping the beliefs and behaviour of individuals. Winslow acknowledges that the primary purpose of military forces, war, is central to their organizational cultures. She notes that small unit cohesion is essential to combat effectiveness, but that, in the cases she studied, organizational norms such as fierce group loyalty interfered with the mission.[66] The Canadian regimental system is based on the British regimental system but with "uniquely Canadian twists," reflecting the linguistic and geographic realities of this country.[67] "A regiment's essence is tribal and corporate rather than instrumental and bureaucratic"; however, the enculturation process used to form group solidarity is a "double-edged sword," according to Winslow.[68] The excessive use of alcohol, often as part of regimental bonding activities, is portrayed as one cause of the problems in the missions under scrutiny. Winslow notes that regiments are powerful entities in the Canadian Army and that they influence the career advancement of their members through semi-official means. Despite the advantages of the corporate nature of regiments, they can have disadvantages as well, including the development of a dysfunctional "we-they" attitude and the development of an attitude of only "looking after their own" among officers.[69]

Winslow concludes that the CF have a long tradition of an organizational culture oriented toward combat effectiveness. This in turn shapes the values and goals of the organization by reinforcing primary group bonding through formal and informal socialization. She notes, however, that the "corporate nature of army culture" can lead to a "sense of exclusiveness" which in extreme cases is used to justify disrespect for authority "outside the group." To avoid the potential dysfunctional effects of misplaced loyalties, the leadership of the CF must ensure that there is a healthy balance between small group loyalty and loyalty to the organization. In the cases cited, leadership at all levels failed to ensure that this balance was maintained.[70]

A wider perspective on Canadian military culture was presented by Bland at a 1999 Conference of Defence Associations Institute seminar. He argued that the CF are resistant to change because of the "persistent and deep-seated idea in the minds of Canadian Forces officers" that "a tri-service organization of the Canadian Forces based on the army, navy, and air force is the preferred structure for the armed forces," and that "in all situations and in all times" it is best for national defence. Noting the "obvious benefit that flows to leaders" of the environmental commands (the land, sea, and air components of the CF, which correspond to the former services – army, navy, and air force),[71] Bland suggests that these leaders "see their main responsibility as protecting and enhancing their particular institutions" in the name of promoting a viable national defence policy. However, this structure "perpetuates redundant missions and institutions, prevents the rational distribution of defence resources, and fuels the inter-service rivalries that at times discredit the armed forces before politicians and senior public service leaders," according to Bland. This situation is exacerbated because senior officers gain promotion within their services by "winning resources" for their particular service. At the same time, Bland tells us that "few senior officers would be so bold as to advocate the dismantling of a rival service, at least overtly," because they understand that "appearing to share scarce resources protects them from criticism." Therefore, slogans such as "balanced forces" or "general purpose forces," with no agreed meaning, are used "to provide a blanket of civility over the ongoing struggle for place and funding between services who are working for their own interests and not necessarily for the interests of national defence."[72]

A critical view of the CF's culture is also taken by Near in a recently published essay. He notes that the "Report on the Leadership and Management of the Canadian Forces" (dated 26 March 1996) and Somalia Commission Report (tabled 30 June 1997) subjected the CF to an unprecedented level of scrutiny and analysis. These reports were described by Near as "seminal and historic" because of the scrutiny and analysis and the wide-ranging reforms they proposed. Between them, the two reports made 225 recommendations, with 134 of these related to "leadership and management."[73] In lamenting the triumph of corporate business practices imposed on the CF by the government for reasons of fiscal management, Near cites Granatstein in saying that the business approach has "triumphed over military virtues." However, a business approach is fundamentally unsuited to defence or any other public service because this approach will erode the "civic virtues and ethos of these institutions."[74]

Near suggests that to be effective the CF needs "a clear, well articulated sense of military purpose" and the CF must be linked to the government and the citizens of the nation in a "symbiotic relationship." He goes on to argue that many of the leadership failures and deficiencies in professionalism of the past ten years can be attributed to the absence of a clear military purpose for the CF since the end of the Cold War and the CF's continued weak links to the "institutions of government" and the Canadian people. Near claims that the CF cannot expect political leaders or taxpayers to support the CF unless the forces are perceived as relevant to the country's needs and subscribe "to values that ordinary Canadians support and admire." He concludes that the erosion of the CF's ethos is due to its lack of clear military purpose and its disconnection from basic Canadian values. To remedy these problems, Near proposes some solutions. One solution is for members of the CF to "see themselves as Canadian citizens first, and military members second," and another is for the CF to have an ethos based on traditional military virtues and a commitment to professional excellence. Unfortunately, Near contends, the current document titled "The Ethos of the Canadian Forces" is only one variant of a plethora of statements about "values, beliefs and ethics" circulating in the CF, and it is neither well known nor embedded anywhere in CF doctrine.[75]

Wild echoes these arguments in his analysis of the Canadian Army's current culture. He argues that the culture and ethos of the army are in conflict, and as a result "mixed messages are received and hidden agendas suspected by soldiers." This has led to soldiers' perceptions of unfairness, arbitrariness, and double standards. Wild also asserts that if the CF, particularly the army, espouse a vocational ethos, then they should look after their members who are injured or hurt; however, the "ethos" of universality of service has led to those who are not fully employable being discharged from the services. This policy plus evidence that the CF have not always looked after their members properly has led those who perhaps once saw the CF as a vocation to see it as merely a job, and not a very appealing one at that. This should not surprise us, Wild contends, because the CF emphasize the personal benefits of joining the CF, enrol people using contractual terms of service, and increasingly pay people according to their skills and knowledge, as opposed to their rank. These occupational inducements to join the CF attract people who see the CF more as a job than a career, and, according to Wild, by paying people according to their skills and knowledge, the CF treat vocations like occupations and occupations like vocations.[76]

Bercuson's examination of Canadian military culture includes his analysis of what attracts people to the military. In the Second World War, the 1.2 million who volunteered for the Canadian Army were motivated by patriotism, unemployment, and the desire to stay with friends, relatives, and classmates who had enlisted. In recent times, most of those who join the CF appear to be motivated by practical considerations: to learn a trade or profession, to advance themselves, or to undertake challenging work. Service to nation is not high in this list of priorities. Until recently, the CF were attracting adequate numbers of recruits, and so the more pertinent question for maintaining an effective military force was, Why do people stay beyond their initial term of service? Some of the answers given by Bercuson were that these people liked the social structure of the armed forces because, as a "highly structured and ordered meritocracy," they provide the companionship and built-in support systems characteristic of some vocations.[77]

The increasingly occupational attitudes of officers in the CF, Wild argues, is a result of a key officer entry program at Canada's only remaining military college – RMC. Cadets are promised occupational benefits, a free education plus pay as a cadet, and a steady job after graduation. In addition, cadets sign contracts for obligatory service after graduation, but contracts are signs of an occupation not a vocation. Claims that RMC has succeeded in instilling military values in its graduates are contradicted by data that show that the retention rate for RMC graduates is no better than that of other officer entry plans.[78]

The increasingly occupational attitudes of the officer corps in the CF have led to behaviour that threatens the trust that subordinates put in their leaders. Wild cites a study by the NCM Professional Development Working Group that found that "NCMs [non-commissioned members] feel they lack the support of an officer corps more concerned with ticket punching than doing their job."[79] Another survey taken in the 1990s found that even though more than two thirds of military personnel were committed to DND as more than just a place to work, there was a widespread lack of confidence in its leadership. Bercuson explains that the crisis of values in the CF arose from the fact that, in today's CF, military virtues are not rewarded as much as the "managerial, ass-covering, political skills that lead to promotion." He says that the Canadian Army's deepest crisis is to ensure that army leaders are first and foremost "true warriors whose morality, integrity, and courage" set the tone for the entire force.[80] One of the few empirical studies in the CF on the subject of leadership and trust in units deployed on operations, in this case on Operation Harmony, revealed that as many as 41 per cent of unit personnel expressed "low confidence" in the leadership of junior officers and that up to 33.8 per cent of unit personnel expressed "low confidence" in the leadership of senior officers. This indicates that there are potentially serious leadership shortcomings in the CF. However, until much more research is done to put these figures in context – e.g., Are these numbers comparable to or better than other military forces or civilian organizations? – they can only serve to alert us to a situation that requires attention.[81] Lack of confidence in leadership has also been manifested by situations where junior and mid-level leaders will not pass bad news up the chain of command because they are afraid that this might reflect badly on their own competence. An inappropriate "can do" attitude, where asking for assistance is perceived to be an "admission of inability," has resulted in some cases.

These findings have widespread implications for the CF: Wild cites a 1995 survey which found that "only 17 per cent of CF personnel had 'confidence in the most senior levels of the Department to lead us through these difficult times.'" Wild also criticizes the "Defence Team" concept as meaningless if uniformed members are expected to be vocational and civilian DND employees to be occupational. Wild concludes that as an institution the CF profess a vocational ethos, but that their culture supports an occupational ethos. He notes that the same "'confusion regarding appropriate role models for military personnel and appropriate military institutions'" noted by Cotton still exist twenty years later.[82] Is this an example of lack of adaptation, as Wild claims, or simply a reflection that there will always be ambiguity and confusion in an era of constant change in society and the military?

CONCLUSIONS

Prior to unification in 1968, the Canadian military culture, like most military cultures in the Western world, was a loose amalgam of the three service (army, navy, and air force) cultures, each with its distinctive aspects. Canada is unique among Western nations in the degree that its armed forces have been unified, and this has created a unique CF culture, while certain aspects of the three service cultures have been perpetuated. On one hand, a number of advantages have accrued to the unified CF, particularly the ability to inculcate a joint atmosphere into many aspects of training and operations. Certain efficiencies have also been realized since the support branches of the three services were integrated. On the other hand, unification has fostered some values and attitudes that are seen by some as antithetical to the military ethos. Most observers believe that since unification the culture of the CF has become more occupational and less vocational. In addition, the bureaucratization and civilianization of DND have led to an ethos within the CF that has focused more on business practices than the virtues of the warrior that are necessary in a military culture. Officers, particularly senior officers, are perceived as being more interested in their careers than in service to the nation. Coupled with downsizing and other personnel policies based on an occupational model, this careerism has transmitted the message throughout the CF that the armed services exist in Canada to provide jobs rather than a vocation or calling. But this message has been competing with exhortations to "service before self" and the truly dedicated performance of most members of the CF in many difficult circumstances. Research by Soeters and Recht that indicates that Canada, along with Norway, leads other armed services on the path toward what the two researchers believe to be the future – a more modern occupational model of military forces – seems to suggest that this path is preferable to returning to traditional vocational values. The result of these mixed messages has been confusion among members of the CF as to what values, attitudes, beliefs, and behaviour they should ascribe to.

Due to this confusion, the CF exhibit many of the same characteristics of a non-adaptive culture that were identified in today's

US military in the previous chapter. Once again a lack of trust seems to have developed between superiors and subordinates, partially due to careerism, an unwarranted "can do" attitude, and evidence of a business ethos on the part of some leaders. The same lack of communication observed in the American armed services, especially a reluctance to pass bad news up the chain of command, appears to exist in the CF as well. And once again we have evidence of cautious leaders who try to protect their own interests by behaving insularly, politically, and bureaucratically, valuing orderly and risk-reducing management processes much more highly than leadership initiatives.[83] As with the US military, the root cause of these problems in the CF seems to be the difference between the organization's espoused values and values-in-use.

Another area of commonality between the CF and the American armed services is the assumption that the CF have a relatively homogeneous culture in terms of ethnicity. This assumption appears to be supported by the CF's current demographics, but, as we shall see shortly, this situation may change in the not too distant future. At this point in time, theories of organizational culture that offer insights into multicultural organizations may well be vital to future research.

All these observations must be tempered, however, by the knowledge that in the case of the CF very little research has been done to support these tentative conclusions. The subject of Canadian military culture remains largely unexplored, with only a relatively few works examining this topic in any detail. This leaves students of Canadian military culture with little certainty in a field of great importance to both the CF and Canadian society. Until a comprehensive study of Canadian military culture is conducted, many of the questions raised here will remain open to answers based on speculation and conjecture.

6

Comparing Military Culture in Canada and the United States

Now that we have reviewed key aspects of Canadian and American military culture, comparing them is arguably the best way to examine the influence of the American military culture on the CF. This will also permit a discussion of two key issues: the inevitability of the absorption and internalization of American military values and ethics by Canadian officers, and the risk of the Americanization of the Canadian officer corps. Before making this comparison, it is necessary to have an understanding of the national cultures which underlie the military cultures. Most readers are familiar with American culture today, but many people are unsure about what exactly constitutes Canadian culture. This comparison of Canadian and American military culture therefore begins with a brief discussion of the nature of Canadian culture and its similarities and differences from American culture.

CANADIAN CULTURE

Canadian culture has often been referred to as a "cultural mosaic." Some recognize the existence of two "founding peoples" represented by the French and British cultures. Others see more of a variety of cultures, including Amerindians, Inuit, and Métis, not to mention the cultures of the many non-British immigrants who flooded this country in the nineteenth and twentieth centuries. For some, the effect of language on Canadian cultural behaviour is a vital question. Anthropologists have found that a person's language is not only an instrument to express ideas; it also affects the way people think about the world. Based on what

Castonguay refers to as the "distinct cultural traits" of anglophones and francophones, he maintains that, despite their similarities, French-speaking and English-speaking officers exhibit different leadership styles. Castonguay claims that Serge Bernier and Jean Pariseau's 1994 book *French Canadians and Bilingualism in the Canadian Armed Forces* contains a "gold mine" of information on the topic. Unfortunately, though Castonguay suggests that lessons learned in the integration of francophones into the CF might well be of help in integrating visible minorities in the future, the mine remains largely unworked due to a lack of subsequent research.[1]

In general terms there are fundamental differences between Canadian and American culture based on differences in geography, climate, demography, and history, according to Pierre Berton. Canadians, even Québécois, have always accepted more government control over their lives than Americans as the price to be paid for security. The settlement of the Canadian West and recent Quebec language laws are held up by Berton as examples of Canadians putting security ahead of civil liberties.[2]

A recent examination of Canadian social values by the Environics Research Group has confirmed Berton's impressions about Canadian culture. The research suggests that Canada has been transformed by a "social revolution" over the past twenty-five years, but that this was a peaceful revolution where Canadians broke away from the stereotypes and roles often imposed by a tiny elite in society and took personal responsibility for defining their values and aspirations. However, the Environics study concludes that while values still matter most in defining a nation, "growing individualism means that the demographic stereotypes of the past are less accurate than ever before." The Canadian consensus on social values may be breaking down as "Canada adopts a 'pull' culture focussed on personal autonomy and self-fulfilment." Adams argues that in our recent history, starting in the 1970s, the definition of a Canadian was "not an American," and that many Canadians were anti-American. There was some rapprochement with the US during the 1980s under Brian Mulroney's Conservative government, but in the 1990s Canada has reverted to a "close enough ... but not too" close relationship with the US. Adams and others have proposed that a new post-modern, English-Canadian nationalism based on the multicultural paradigm is developing. More and more, they claim, English-speaking Canadians are adopting what Adams calls "multiple identities and flexible personalities." The behaviour of these Canadians can no longer be adequately explained by the traditional categories of geography (where people live) and demographics (including ethnic origins). Where Canadians were once defined by their race, religion, or region, they now define themselves by their values, personal priorities, and life choices. "Demography is no longer destiny," they claim. This is in contrast to the US where demographic factors, especially race, still strongly determine "values, lifestyles, and opportunities." Adams argues that Canadians "feel strongly about our relatively weak attachments to each other" and that we prefer the understated Canadian version of nationalism to the "in-your-face" nationalism of other countries, particularly our American neighbours' brand of nationalism. Québécois also accept this logic because they see Canadian federalism as a bulwark against economic depression, civil unrest, and violence. In fact the Environics study found that "basic values do not separate French and English Canadians." Adams concludes that "Canadians, like people everywhere, have changed in ways that reflect American and global influences," but that they have done so in a uniquely Canadian way. We have developed a "distinctly Canadian world-view" based on our social values and the institutions we have created to reflect them.[3]

If we accept that future changes in the CF's culture will be significantly affected by changes in Canadian society at large – which is being "Americanized" at an ever increasing rate according to many Canadians – then an important question becomes, Exactly what is "Americanization" and how will it influence our society in the future? For some scholars, "Americanization" is "an evolving idea, an ever-changing matrix of cultural beliefs and practices that arose within the borders of what is now the United States, but which also is filtered through other cultures" in what is often termed *globalization*.[4] Others believe that there is a "central paradox" in the relationship between Canada and the US because "we continue to grow ever more alike but no closer together," and that the key to understanding this relationship is the "interplay of regionalism and borderlands."[5] In fact, Thomas Courchene, an influential public policy advisor at Queen's

University, has suggested that North America may eventually regroup itself around regional trading partnerships and that the nation-state could diminish in importance.[6] The theoretical possibilities of cultural convergence or divergence between Canada and the US notwithstanding, there is empirical evidence that there are cultural differences between American and Canadian business managers, a group that one might expect to be culturally very similar. A recent study has demonstrated that Canadian and American managers cannot be considered "interchangeable" because there are "significant cognitive process preference differences between them." For example, Canadians managers were found to be "more theoretical and imaginative problem solvers" than Americans, a difference that also seems to exist between Canadian and American officer cadets.[7] Little research has been done in this area, but it appears that the American military tends to work more "by the book" than the CF and that a "zero defects" mentality still persists in the US military culture despite the well-known drawbacks of this approach.[8] Therefore, it seems that for all the similarities between the two countries, there are discernible differences between Canadians and Americans, including military officers.

Perhaps the greatest difference today is the enthusiasm that Canadians and the CF, especially the army, have shown for peacekeeping missions. These "non-traditional" military missions have been a part of the Canadian military culture for over forty years. The result has been that in the Canadian public's perception Canada's military personnel are often seen as heroic peacekeepers, as distinct from their American counterparts, who are seen as traditional war fighters.[9] This distinction may explain why the US military, especially the US Army, has stubbornly resisted non-traditional missions. A recent article in the US press described the army's attitude this way: "The heavy-metal faction in the Army has no enthusiasm for playing globo-cop [peacekeeping roles] ... Army training and doctrine are still focused on a massive armored battle. Incredibly, at a time when Army chiefs were calling for speed and mobility, the average armored division grew heavier-by some 20 percent since 1989 ... [There is] a 'pretty passionate' debate in the leadership between the futurists and the 'barons,' the old-line tankers and artillerymen who still dominate the Army's command structure."[10] It has been suggested that US strategic culture is quite permissive in the latitude it provides for the employment of force in support of national objectives, but that peace enforcement and peacekeeping missions, by virtue of their inability to achieve "success" or "decisive" results, will be opposed by many Americans.[11] Most commentators contend that a military organization's roles, missions, and tasks have a vital impact on its culture.[12] The central role of most military forces is to wage war, and this purpose "orients all the basic assumptions, spirit, beliefs, and the characteristic ways of doing things" in the military organization.[13] While combat may be the foundation of military culture, the superstructure varies from force to force, even within nations, depending on the type of war the organization is preparing to wage. In addition, certain military cultures, Canada's for example, put greater emphasis on such activities as peacekeeping and aid to the civil power than do others, the US military culture for example.

INDIVIDUAL SERVICE CULTURE

Another important factor to consider when comparing the military cultures of Canada and the US is that each culture consists of subcultures based on the three Canadian services (army, navy, air force) and the US services (army, navy, air force, and marines). Distinct service cultures exist for good reason – they reflect unique traditions that enhance esprit de corps and facilitate functional specialization.[14] While these subcultures cause divisions in the overall national military culture, they also build bridges between Canadian and American servicemen and servicewomen who work in the same environments. For example, air force transport pilots in Canada and the US may have more in common professionally than they would have with infantry officers in their own armies. The same could be said for many occupations in the services of both countries.

The culture of the US services has received some attention from researchers. For example, Carl Builder, a leading American analyst of the US defence establishment, asserted that the US Army, Navy, and Air Force have "distinct and enduring personalities," and that despite minor evolutionary changes these personalities would remain essentially stable "for a very long time."[15] He described the differences among the American services as follows. The touchstone of the US Army's organizational culture is the art of war and the profession of arms; in other words, concepts and doctrine are the glue that unifies the army's separate branches. For the US Navy, the heart of its organizational culture is the navy as an institution based on tradition and maritime strategy that provide coherence and direction to the navy. The US Air Force, Builder asserted, has in contrast identified with platforms and air weapons rooted in a commitment to technical superiority, and it has transformed aircraft or systems into ends in themselves. Builder claimed this lack of an air force vision has had serious repercussions for the US Air Force. Writing in the early 1990s, Builder maintained that, because the US Air Force had no integrating vision like the US Army's AirLand Battle or the US Navy's Maritime Strategy, it had conceded the intellectual high ground to the other services, particularly the Army.[16] Builder does not discuss the US Marine Corps culture in detail, but it has been described as worshipping "at the altar of its uniqueness," and because of its unique roles it has not been as strongly affected by the end of the Cold War as the other US services have been.[17]

The Center for Strategic and International Studies (CSIS) study, often citing Builder, described the US service cultures in a way similar to his framework. The CSIS report portrayed the army as worshipping at the altar of "service to nation." It also noted that the army has a higher representation of minority groups than the other services with 40 per cent of the active army and 21 per cent its officer corps coming from minority populations. The US Air Force is described as worshipping at the "altar of technology" and as being composed of a number of communities generally grouped around weapons platforms or aircraft types. The US Air Force has integrated women in greater numbers than the other services with 18 per cent of air force personnel being female and 99.7 per cent of air force jobs open to women. The US Navy worships at the "altar of tradition" in this analogy and it is primarily a federation of three war-fighting communities: surface, subsurface, and aviation. It is portrayed as having a fierce streak of independence which, while ensuring its professionalism, insulates it more from social trends and influences. The United States Marine Corps (USMC), according to the CSIS study, has the strongest service culture and it actively discourages subcultures based on branches or "separate war-fighting communities." With its unique amphibious warfare mission go unique personnel policies that have resulted in there being relatively few female marines (they make up only 6 per cent of the USMC).[18]

SERVICE CULTURE AND BEHAVIOUR

There is a dearth of research on the effects of service culture on behaviour; however, Smith's analysis of changes in the organizational culture of the US Air Force provides some insights into this relationship. According to Smith, the US Army is the most closely integrated of the US services. This is attributed to "inter-branch mobility across careers," multi-branch bases, and the fact that the army operates as a combined-arms team, with each specialty interacting with and depending upon the others. Smith notes that current research does not address the US Marine Corps, but that it appears to be even more cohesive than the US Army because of its narrow mission, small size, and integrated organization. Smith describes the US Navy as the second most cohesive of the three services: he claims that its operational interdependence provides a binding force across weapon systems and specialties, and that this cohesion is reinforced through multispecialty interaction in ports and wardrooms. The US Air Force is described as the least cohesive of the services because of the specialized nature of its technologies, the specialization of its wing structure (wings are organized by aircraft/weapon type), and the relative isolation of each specialized unit from the others. Smith asserts that due to these differences each armed service has to find its own unique solutions to the problems of defining and changing organizational culture, and that the US Air Force may need to look outside the military "into other complex government agencies and civilian organizations for models."[19]

True organizational change, Smith continues, requires a cultural transformation which includes changes in professional incentives, behaviours, and structures. Both internal and external factors contribute to change. For example, the US Air Force's role during and after the Cold War led to gradual changes in its culture when the decline of the manned bomber as a nuclear deterrent force saw the rise of new elites in that service who prescribed new cultural norms. But it took until 1997 for the old

Strategic Air Command bomber pilot elite to be replaced by the Tactical Air Command fighter pilot elite at the top levels of the air force. This resulted in internal changes as the "fighter mafia" exerted its influence. The US Air Force, according to Smith, is now using its new vision of "Global Engagement," to compete with the other US services for scarce resources.[20]

Smith provides empirical evidence to show that higher rank and increased professional military education result in a more institutional (versus occupational) attitude in officers. He concludes that this means an infrastructure exists upon which to build US Air Force cohesion. Smith describes a process for effecting organizational change which includes the three steps of (1) defining the new vision of the force, (2) realigning strategy and structure to the vision, and (3) changing the organizational culture to reflect the vision. This process is unique to each service in the US armed forces, and by extension unique to the CF's environments as well. However, according to Smith, for the process to work the "officer corps must share essential values, define the service core mission(s) within the operational and political environments, create a unifying vision, and undertake strategic planning and action to promulgate that vision."[21]

THE NEW "JOINT" CULTURE

Among new cultures and visions, the emergence of a fifth culture – a joint culture – has been commented upon in the American literature recently. The 1986 Goldwater-Nichols Department of Defense Reorganization Act started what has become a case study in how legislation can achieve effective cultural change in the US military, according to the CSIS report. The act mandated jointness in the US armed forces, and in theory the American military vision of the future is guided by this act and a series of documents supporting "Joint Vision 2010" (published in June 1996) and updated by "Joint Vision 2020"(published in May 2000). The key effects of Goldwater-Nichols were (1) to make the chairman of the Joint Chiefs of Staff the principal military advisor to the Secretary of Defense and the President; (2) to enhance the powers of unified commanders in the field (the CINCs or regional Commanders-in-Chief, now called Combatant Commanders);[22] and (3) to increase the significance of joint assignments for senior military officers by making joint duty a requirement for promotion to flag or general officer rank. This has resulted in a new joint culture emerging at field-grade and senior officer levels, suggesting the evolution of multiple military cultures and the increasing dominance of the officer subculture over other subcultures in the American military.[23]

Despite the advantages of a new joint culture for military operations, there is reason to be cautious about the most optimistic claims for "jointness." At the moment, joint culture still suffers from "cultural schizophrenia" based on its historical roots. After its poor performance in Vietnam, the US Army underwent an intellectual renaissance that continues to this today. One of the key ideas to arise from this renaissance was a focus on the operational level of war: from this focus there emerged an emphasis on operational art centred on land warfare as the key to victory.[24] This led to the US Army's quest, supported in some aspects by the USMC, for the predominance of its vision of joint warfare. This vision was accepted by the US Joint Chiefs of Staff and enunciated in 1996 in "Joint Vision 2010."The idea that a "joint" vision might not be a unifying concept or that there could be different ideas of what "joint" warfare should be in practice can be difficult to grasp, but as Elinor Sloan argues, there are a number of problems in achieving the jointness legislated by Goldwater-Nichols. For example, there is little focused effort on joint experimentation activities and over 90 per cent of US military experimentation is carried out by the services individually. Furthermore, the "dominant military service cultures" continue to focus on legacy equipment, which is reflected in procurement budgets that do not fully reflect service visions. Finally, there is resistance to the changes required in the Joint Vision documents by some in the US Air Force and US Navy who feel these documents were and remain a thinly disguised attempt by the army to gain pre-eminence among the services, and to relegate the air force and navy to support roles on the battlefield.[25] This view was graphically described by General Anthony C. Zinni (USMC, retired), a former Commander-in-Chief of US Central Command: "We teach our [junior officers] to recognize that sister service as the enemy ... we fight each other for money, programs, and weapon systems. We try to out-doctrine each other by putting pedantic little anal apertures ... in doctrine centers ... to ace out the other services and become the dominant service in some way … Interservice rivalry … [is] going to kill us if we don't find a better way to do business."[26]

Yet, some American commentators have claimed that there are advantages to inter-service competition because intra-service secrecy is exposed by the other services, disunity gives civilian authorities leverage if the armed services do not present a unified front, and competition among the services spurs innovation and provides multiple perspectives on defence issues.[27] These considerations are particularly important to those in the US who accept Builder's hypothesis that the US armed services have become the most powerful institutions in the American national security arena and that the military has become too independent of civilian control.[28] Whatever the advantages or disadvantages of closer integration of the US services, it has been pointed out that despite the "jointness" mandated by the Goldwater-Nichols Act, the US services still maintain their own separate academies, uniforms, staff and affiliated civilian secretariat, and a continuing attachment to certain weapons systems. And in the most recent large-scale conflict to be exhaustively analysed in the literature, the Gulf War in 1991, each pursued its own strategy.[29]

IMPACT ON THE CF

The disparity in the organizational cultures of the US armed services has had a significant impact on the CF. Despite the fact that a unified CF would seem to be ideally suited to the integrated approach to modern warfare advocated by "Joint Vision 2010,"the major impact of unification in 1968 was upon the bureaucratic organization of the CF and DND, and there was relatively little impact in terms of joint operations.[30] Throughout the Cold War, despite "common uniforms and common rank designation" brought about by unification, the environments of the CF (the former three services) continued to carry out the same functions with the same equipment as the previously separate services had done. There was no comprehensive plan for the elements of the CF to act together as a joint force, and maritime, land, and air formations and units were assigned to NATO or other higher formations piecemeal.[31] Furthermore, instead of creating its own unified or joint doctrine, since the beginning of the Cold War the

CF have had an "obsession" with American defence interests and doctrine.[32] The Canadian Air Force has been particularly closely associated with the US Air Force and has adopted most of the latter's doctrine and philosophy unreservedly.[33] The Canadian Navy also has close ties to its US analogue because the US Navy "has become the 'industry standard' against which all aspects of naval capability are measured." From the Canadian Navy's point of view, even if its forces participate in some form of a coalition without the US Navy, the common ground among those forces that do participate will normally be their compatibility with America's navy.[34] The Canadian Army has had a somewhat different relationship with the US Army than the other two Canadian services with their American counterparts. Canada's army has been part of the group of Western armies that has enthusiastically accepted recent US Army doctrinal initiatives.[35] And like these armies, the Canadian Army puts a heavy emphasis on doctrine (more so than the navy or air force), and, it hs therefore been the main author of most CF "joint" doctrine. In writing this doctrine, the Canadian Army has applied many recent US Army concepts, even though it has modified some of the doctrine based on its own experience since the Second World War.[36] Therefore, like US joint doctrine, much of the terminology used in Canadian joint doctrine is "land-centric." This creates some problems in the integration of the doctrine used by each of the three environmental compoments of the CF (land, sea, and air) with CF joint doctrine, as expressed in the CF operations manual (*Canadian Forces Operations)*. For example, the "land-centric" definitions of deployability and sustainment do not coincide very well with the operational nature of ships. Consequently, the Maritime Command publication, "Adjusting Course: A Naval Strategy for Canada" and Air Command's "Out of the Sun: Aerospace Doctrine for the Canadian Forces," while broadly consistent with the CF operations manual, lack a direct connection for joint interoperability. Instead, they reflect separate environmental component requirements, much like separate service requirements are reflected in US service doctrine.[37] Consequently, the nature of the tasks and missions of the CF exhibit a predominately, though not entirely, combined flavour. Even apparently "joint" domestic operations, such as "Operation Assistance" (the Manitoba flooding crisis of 1997), were not the epitome of a joint operation. Besides numerous problems with communications and doctrine, the air force (true to its doctrinal roots) expressed a preference for centralized (i.e., component or air force) control of air resources as opposed to the control of air assets by the joint force commander (in this case an army officer).[38] From the maritime perspective, a senior naval officer denied that "Operation Assistance" was a joint operation because "A sailor navigating a rubber boat through a wheatfield while reporting to a Land Force brigade commander during the Winnipeg floods is scarcely a joint achievement."[39]

The environmental components of the CF, like the services they replaced, do not always operate very willingly or very effectively together. However, as one senior Canadian officer put it,

> This is not to say that they are deliberately uncooperative. The officers and non-commissioned members of the CF share much in terms of common training and experience. From basic training through junior and senior leadership courses and the Canadian Forces College to service in the integrated National Defence Headquarters, all this reinforces a common CF point of view. So there is an important start to creating the right culture; however, 'there remains much to be done in the areas of command and control, the organisation of infrastructure and joint warfare training.' ... Although there have nominally been 'joint operations' since the end of the Cold War, in reality these have been single environmental components, land, sea, and air components, reporting to a national contingent commander. The components themselves have been subsumed in larger multinational maritime, land and air formations.

Despite many exhortations for increased "jointness" among the CF's land, sea, and air components, Canadian participation in the Gulf War was typical of the Canadian armed services' historical propensity for serving as adjuncts to larger allied services but separate from the other Canadian services or environmental components.[40] Therefore, the greatest force for the adoption of foreign doctrine and philosophy in the CF and "Americanization" in the CF's officer corps would appear to be the desire for interoperability by each of the Canadian environments with their American counterparts rather than the impetus of any overarching American joint vision.

This is not necessarily a bad thing, given the state of current American and NATO joint doctrine. A number of Canadian and foreign officers who have studied joint doctrine extensively have cautioned us that because allied joint doctrine "contains serious flaws" and may have been written to resolve national service issues that are not necessarily problems in Canada, we should avoid the current practice of importing large amounts of unmodified foreign joint doctrine.[41] Ongoing CF initiatives to create a Joint Force Headquarters and to refine CF joint doctrine, plus the fact that the CF are legally an integrated and unified force, have the potential to resolve many of the issues that other militaries are addressing through their own joint doctrine.[42] However, the historical record is not encouraging in this respect, as the unification and integration of the CF did not alter pre-existing commitments that sent, and often continue to send, the environmental components of the CF in different directions. Not only had Canada's three armed services never fought as a national force before unification in 1968, they have not done so since.[43] The present state of affairs suggests that tension will persist between a desire to implement truly joint CF doctrine with roles for the three environmental components of the CF to operate together and their desire to remain up-to-date, combat-capable forces, which implies close ties with the culturally diverse American armed services.

WHY AMERICAN RESEARCH ON MILITARY CULTURE MAY NOT APPLY TO THE CF

As useful as the data from the many American studies on military culture are, Okros has suggested that many of the findings may not be transferable to the study of Canadian military culture. He notes that there is congruence within each nation about the degree that each country's military should accommodate social change, but there are significant differences between countries. For example, Americans are prepared to accept limits on the civil rights of those serving in uniform, while Canadians are not.[44]

Core assumptions underlying American research may not apply in the Canadian context, Okros contends, including the seminal Huntington-Janowitz models concerning military professionalism and civil-military relations. He offers a number of reasons to explain this, some of which follow. The first reason is based on the role and nature of the government and military in the two contexts. Americans accept that their overriding foreign policy objective is to pursue the nation's interests, whereas Canadians are prepared to countenance the establishment of an international governance structure to support human security which subordinates national interests to the international common good where required. Secondly, Americans believe that government should only do for citizens what they cannot do for themselves, whereas Canadians believe that government should concern itself with maintaining social cohesion, national standards for a social safety net, and protecting cultural sovereignty. Next, many Americans understand that the nation's military has a primary role of winning wars, whereas the vast majority of Canadians are happy with a minimum military capability as the price of membership in regional and international organizations. Okros also argues that the American model of the dyad of military and society is not applicable in Canada, where there are more players and the military must be many things to many people. In these circumstances, it is critical for the CF to align its culture, values, and behaviour with human rights principles espoused by the majority of Canadians. The tolerable gap between military culture and human rights principles for the war-fighting model often embraced in the US is intolerable under the soldier-diplomat human-security-force model adopted by Canada.[45]

As we have seen, Okros's arguments seem to have some validity. Since unification the CF have gradually adopted most of the norms of Canadian society and have now explicitly claimed a "critical role" in promoting not only Canadian values but also Canada's economic well-being."[46] From official bilingualism to the acceptance of gays and lesbians in the military, the CF have often been on the leading edge of change in Canadian society. One interpretation of this phenomenon is that it "reflects a deeper part of the Canadian social and cultural tradition" that is also present in the military.[47]

A COMPARISON OF THE CANADIAN AND US ARMED SERVICES

There are clear differences between the US and Canadian armed services which need not be repeated in detail here. Based on the experience of the past sixty years, the American way of war has relied on large, usually conscript-based armed forces – guided by politicians (most of whom had served in the military) – fighting conventional wars, using mass and American technology to attempt to inflict decisive defeat on the enemy. Perhaps the greatest difference between the Canadian and American militaries during this time period is that the vast majority of those who served in Canada's armed forces, even in the two world wars, were volunteers.[48] Another important difference is that, since the Second World War, most Canadian military operations have been in support of UN or other peace operations. Yet, recently, the similarities between the military forces of the two nations have been increasing.

The American military since the end of the Cold War has begun to resemble, in some respects, the Canadian military in both its composition and missions. This has the potential to cause a convergence in organizational cultures, but in ways not often articulated. On one hand, the attitudes of senior American decision-makers toward military service has been coloured by their long experience with the draft between 1942 and 1973. On the other hand, as Cotton put it, "the essential character of the Canadian military ethos" is that for most of our history military service has been a voluntary act.[49] Only recently has the US begun to accept the necessity of a small (by American standards) volunteer force, and the US is just now coming to grips with issues related to this new force structure that the Canadian military has struggled with for many years. For example, a reliance on reservists to sustain regular force missions is a reality that has been faced by the Canadian military since its earliest days. A relatively new phenomenon for the American military, this reliance on reservists has transformed the US military to the point where national guard and reserve soldiers actually outnumber those in the regular US Army – 564,000 to 479,000. And in the last ten years, reservists' time on active duty supporting military operations has risen from one million days to nearly 13 million.[50]

With the advent of the all-volunteer force, the average age of American forces members has increased and more are married than in the conscripted forces of the past (fewer than 10 per cent of draftees were married compared to more than 30 per cent of corporals in 1998),[51] and unprecedented numbers of women are serving in the US forces, some of them in non-traditional jobs.

This older and more mixed gender force has higher expectations of quality of life and job satisfaction and a more occupational, rather than vocational, approach to military service. American forces, like the CF have been for most of the twentieth century, are now in widespread competition with civilian society for recruits. With the disappearance of the draft, many of today's American youth, like their Canadian counterparts, do not perceive joining the military as an attractive option.[52]

Another similarity between the CF and the US armed services that has come to the fore since the end of the Cold War is the debate over the primary mission of the armed forces. The professional ethos of the US military has traditionally centred on combat, but it is now conceded by most observers that peace support and other similar operations other than war are essential to US national interests. At the same time, it is argued that these types of missions are affecting the combat readiness of the armed forces and causing uncertainty about the essential combat focus of US military forces.[53] As we have seen, this is an issue the CF has been struggling with for at least forty years. The US forces, despite some legal restraints, have also become more involved in domestic roles, an activity in which the Canadian military has had a long tradition of participation.[54] Another consequence of the end of the draft is that the US military is now having to deal with a political elite that is increasingly lacking in military experience, a situation the CF has accepted for most of the twentieth century.

US forces recently experienced another "Canadian" phenomenon – massive downsizing. From its Cold War peak of 2.6 million, the US active duty force has been reduced to 1.4 million, a cut of some 46 per cent. Spending on defence in the US has also declined dramatically from 6 per cent of gross national product (GNP) in the mid-1980s to less than 3 per cent ten years later.[55] The post–Cold War CF has always been squeezed for resources, both personnel and financial. In terms of GNP, defence spending has usually been around 2 per cent or less; recently it has been down to its lowest point since the 1930s at 1.5 per cent of GNP.[56] From a Cold War peak of over 100,000, the CF regular force is now under 60,000, a decrease of over 40 per cent.[57] The recent capability-commitment gap experienced by US forces has long been a fact of life for the CF, but recent pressures due to increased operational tempo are something the CF seems to have experienced at about the same time as the American forces.

The treatment of women and homosexuals is another experience shared by the armed services of both nations. The policy of the US military toward the employment of women in combat roles during the Cold War was exclusionary. Most of the integration of women into the US services, especially in non-traditional roles, occurred in the 1990s. The policy on employing homosexuals in the American armed services is ambiguous and a matter of considerable debate. The "don't ask, don't tell" policy introduced in 1994 to accommodate homosexual participation in the US military has actually resulted in an increase in discharges for homosexuality by about 40 per cent.[58] The CF have dealt with similar issues but are generally ahead of the US military in willingness to accommodate societal norms. Women comprise about 11 per cent of the CF regular force and were first deployed on peacekeeping operations in 1973. All combat occupations, except service on submarines, were opened to women in the CF after a human rights tribunal ruling in 1989. Homosexuals have been enrolled and retained in the CF since October 1992, and this has apparently had no negative impact in areas critics of this policy believed it would.[59] This lack of negative impact has recently been confirmed by the British armed forces, which only lifted their ban on gays in the military in 2000.[60] The overall picture in treatment of women and homosexuals shows that once again Canada has led the US in the implementation of policies that moved toward societal norms and away from traditional military attitudes.

In terms of "jointness," the CF have had joint officer education for all three services at RMC since it reopened after the Second World War, and joint basic training for all service members since unification in the late 1960s. Joint senior officer education started with National Defence College in 1948 and was extended with the joint Command and Staff Course phased in between 1966 and 1974 as part of the integration and unification of the CF.[61] Today, virtually all basic and high level training and education is conducted in a "joint" atmosphere. As we have seen, these joint experiences have not necessarily led to any joint operational capability in the CF. On the other hand, the practice of making service cultures more compatible is an issue where the CF experience predates the American experience by some twenty years.

THE CANADIANIZATION OF THE AMERICAN MILITARY

There is no doubt that the CF have been Americanized to some extent. The desire for interoperability by each of the three environmental components of the CF services with their American counterparts, as reinforced by government policy, is perhaps the most potent influence. In addition, the close similarities between American and Canadian popular culture act as catalysts to this process. However, from the trends discussed above there is evidence suggesting that there have been changes in the American military culture that might lead to the US forces becoming more "Canadianized." American forces seem to be going toward the Canadian model of military service: relatively small all-volunteer professional forces directed by politicians who not only have never served in the armed forces of their country but who are largely ignorant of military affairs in general. American forces have also been called upon to participate in operations ranging from humanitarian aid to conventional war, while constrained by shrinking resources. Like their Canadian counterparts, the American services have been compelled by government legislation and policies to employ groups that were previously excluded from or marginalized in the military on the basis of race, gender, and/or sexual orientation. Based on these factors the armed forces of the US could be described as becoming Canadianized. As unlikely as it may seem to many that Canadian culture could influence the US, no less a personage than John Kenneth Galbraith has maintained that this is precisely what has happened in some instances. Born in Canada but an American citizen since 1937, Galbraith argues that Canadian initiatives on a wide variety of international and social issues have influenced the views that Americans, especially American liberals, hold on some of these issues. Galbraith claims that the "Canadian experience, if not perfect, was clearly better" in some areas, like foreign and military policy where Canada presented viable alternatives to US policy for Americans to consider.[62]

From a military perspective, the small size of the CF gives them the agility and flexibility to react to change more quickly than the American armed services. The close ties the CF have with the US military also give the CF the ability to share their experiences with change in an atmosphere of trust and collegiality. The CF may be in a position, therefore, to exert an inordinate influence on their larger neighbour. However, too often when DND personnel use terms like *interoperability* and *co-operation*, the implication is that it is the CF that must always adopt US methods. This may not always be a wise course of action, and the next chapter will examine what consequences these tendencies might have for the future of the Canadian and American forces.

7

The Future

The future of the culture of the CF and its officer corps will be determined by a number of factors whose effects are not entirely clear. This chapter will discuss some issues that are likely to have an impact on whether American military values and ethics will be absorbed and internalized by Canadian officers and whether a Canadian military culture can exist in the twenty-first century. The influence of technology on warfare, formulated in the expression "Revolution in Military Affairs," is expected by many today to be the dominant influence on change in the militaries of the world in the coming century. Moreover, as we have seen, DND has committed itself to integrate "the application of RMA-based concepts" into its programs, especially in the realm of command and leadership; the RMA will therefore be the first factor to be examined. This will be followed by a discussion of the future influence of the two factors of operations other than war and Canadian civil culture on Canadian, and where applicable American, military culture.

THE DEBATE OVER THE REVOLUTION IN MILITARY AFFAIRS

Over the last ten years, the term "Revolution in Military Affairs" has dominated debate over the future of warfare. As the US has become the paramount technological and military power in the world, Canadian decision-makers have accepted that the CF must be interoperable with US forces, both technically and doctrinally. Consequently, the concept of an RMA is critical to answering some of the questions relating to the Americanization of the CF posed at the beginning of this book. This is particularly true since many senior decision-makers in the CF have accepted that the CF must embrace the US-led RMA. However, before proceeding further, it is necessary to understand more about the nature of the RMA and its potential effects on warfare in the future.

The Revolution in Military Affairs is currently defined by the US Office of Net Assessment as "a major change in the nature of warfare brought about by the innovative application of new technologies which, combined with dramatic changes in military doctrine and operational and organizational concepts, fundamentally alter the character and conduct of military operations."[1] This definition includes factors such as doctrine and organization, but technology is pre-eminent because today's RMA-based "orthodoxy about future warfare holds that precision air and missile strikes will dominate future warfare and that the struggles for information supremacy will replace the breakthrough battle as the decisive issue for success."[2]

Some advocates of the RMA have taken this interpretation even further. Admiral William A. Owens, a leading proponent of the RMA, claimed in his 1995 book *High Seas: The Naval Passage to an Uncharted World* that American forces could be given near invincibility in future wars through the use of "immune power projection based on a family of stand-off, precision-guided, weapons, as well as space and electronic-warfare capabilities and ballistic-missile defenses."[3] This fits in well with the American way of war as reiterated by a former chief of staff of the US Army in 1997: "Only through decisive victory or the undisputed ability to achieve it can US national interests be assured." Even though he cautioned that "we cannot eliminate the irrational aspects of war through a purely technical solution," most of the acolytes of the RMA have ignored this caveat.[4]

Many of the ideas upon which the concept of the RMA is based came from the books *War and Anti-War* published in 1993 and *The Third Wave* by Alvin and Heidi Toffler published in 1980.[5] The spread of the Tofflers' ideas was helped by their connections in high political and military circles and the fact that their subject appealed to a military audience hungry for a leading-edge discussion of their profession. However, the Tofflers' claim that software will triumph over steel in future wars has been challenged on a number of fronts, especially by those who feel that they have neglected the human aspect of the human-technology interface and that their analysis of the historical record has been superficial. In many ways their arguments are based on economic determinism – "the way we make war reflects the way we make wealth" – arguing that a third historic economic transformation, based on knowledge, is underway. As Steven Metz put it, "Quintessentially American, the Tofflers concentrate on technology feasibility with little concern for the strategic, political, social, psychological or even ethical implications of changing military technology." Metz goes on to critique the Tofflers' approach because it postulates that technology is driving and shaping history and tends to neglect the effect of human values and systems of organization. In doing so, they have bent history to fit their model of economic causality. While Metz sees the popularity of Tofflers' book in the US military as understandable, he contends that the ubiquity of the acceptance of its concepts is worrisome.[6]

Martin van Creveld offers a competing explanation about the nature of future war. He turns the causal relationship around and argues that how and why people fight help to determine their political, economic, and even social organization. He argues that, for some, war is not always a means to achieve a goal, but an end in itself, a highly attractive activity for which no other can provide an adequate substitute due to the status, riches, and power gained through war. Van Creveld advances the profoundly radical idea that armed forces as they are presently organized and the territorial states that nurture them are obsolete and will fade away, and that all armed forces will eventually move toward a guerrilla, irregular configuration. These conclusions run counter to much of the thinking within the US Army (and US Air Force) concerning the use of technology in the wars of the future, but he notes that modern weapons are often useless in operations other than war (OOTW) because these weapons are designed to fight each other. Their complexity means that they work best in the relatively uncluttered domains of space, air, and desert and that they do not work well in complicated environments – e.g., urban areas – because they cannot tell friend from foe. We have seen the results of this, van Creveld claims, because since 1945 instead of war being conducted by states, most conflict, from Sri Lanka to

Northern Ireland, has been orchestrated by organizations without a clear territorial base. It has been perpetrated instead by small, concealed, dispersed groups of terrorists who cannot be targeted easily by modern technology. Van Creveld predicts that, in the future, war will be fought not to pursue national interests, but to kill enemy leaders, to convert opponents to one's religion, to obtain booty, or for simple entertainment.[7]

Prior to 1991, the concept of "military revolution" was applied to pre–twentieth century military history which depicted the most significant changes in warfare as occurring gradually. The fundamental question in the RMA debate today, according to many commentators, is whether or not the world is experiencing a *revolution* or a continued evolution in military affairs.[8] To answer this question, Baumann uses the concepts of the paradigm and paradigm shift to look at how we interpret events today. He asks if the American way of war has undergone a paradigm shift, or, in other words, if it has changed fundamentally.

If we look around the globe, according to Baumann, we see nothing unprecedented in the way war is being waged.[9] Nationalist, religious, and ethnic conflicts are hardly a distinctive late twentieth century phenomenon. In fact, Cohen argues that warfare in the Middle Ages might be the most useful analogy for future warfare. As in medieval times, sovereignty does not reside exclusively in states, but is diffused among political, civic, and religious bodies. Warfare then, as now, also involved private entities such as religious orders and private individuals, like the former businessman Osama bin Laden who is said to have a personal fortune of $300 million. Then, as now, military technology varied widely among combatants, from English bowmen and knights, the Arab warriors of Saladin, the Mongol cavalry of Genghis Khan, to the pike-welding peasantry of Switzerland. The relative strength of these warriors defied comparison because their strength varied greatly depending on where and with whom they were fighting.[10] So, Baumann co ntends, if we are in the midst of an RMA we can make a strong case that it has been unfolding for a long time.[11]

Another criticism of the current tendency in many Western armed forces to embrace technology uncritically is put forward by van Creveld in his 1991 book *Technology and War*. In it he argued that technology and war operate on logics that are not only different but actually opposed. Technology rests on precisely known principles, whereas war remains paradoxical and unpredictable. Although war is permeated and governed by technology, it is not entirely responsive to technical solutions alone, especially in cases where opponents are roughly equal. As Jack English put it, organizational capacity has always counted for as much or more than technical development in the history of war.[12]

O'Connell made a similar argument, claiming that the human mind has a deep need to create order out of the chaos of war and weapons therefore tend to be viewed in a manner which makes their effects most calculable. O'Connell goes on to say that beneath the facade of printouts and statistics, most fundamental decisions about weapons are primarily reflections of human motives and considerations – for example, a real navy needs large surface ships, an air force is not an air force without manned fighters, and real armies need tanks. The preference of most western militaries for large, high-tech weapons systems, according to this interpretation, not only preserves existing military organizational cultures but is also key to societal stability because arms are closely bound up with a society's ritual and culture, as well as its economic and political reality. There is often resistance to real change in weaponry because fundamental changes in arms mean a restructuring of society itself. Following this logic, perhaps RMA should stand for the "Reaction in Military Affairs" because its biggest supporters are those who wish to preserve the expensive high-tech status quo.[13]

Jack English characterizes the development of a functioning bureaucracy (begun in the sixteenth century) as the most important military innovation in the early evolution of modern European armies. He and other commentators see national conscription – "the nation in arms" – decreed by French Revolutionary leaders on 23 August 1791 as the greatest political and military transformation the world had yet seen. Likewise, he believes that the greatest military innovation of the nineteenth century was not technological but organizational, as embodied in the institution of the general staff.[14]

However, it was in the First World War, sometimes described as a watershed transformation of war, where all these factors came together. In this conflict, according to English, we see the roots of modern staff planning, indirect fire, air operations of all types, chemical warfare, extensive use of electronic communications, and mechanization. And at the end of the First World War, as in subsequent large wars, success in battle depended on the orchestration of arms and mobility. But a corrective for the admirers of manoeuvre as a key component of future warfare can be found in the results of this new type of mobile "manoeuvre" warfare. Recent scholarship has shattered the myth of the high casualties of the First World War being the exclusive result of trench warfare. For example, the highest casualty rates suffered by the Canadian Corps occurred during the mobile warfare phase of the last "Hundred Days" of the war. The 45,830 casualties the corps incurred between Amiens and Mons represented 20 per cent of the Canadian Expeditionary Force total for the entire war and was more than the 44,735 casualties suffered by the Canadian Army in the Northwest Europe campaign in the Second World War. Nonetheless, the myth that technical means, such as tanks and aircraft, can reduce casualties has persisted to the present, even though there was no discernable reduction in casualties when tanks were used in abundance by both sides in the Second World War. The carnage of the Western front in the First World War only shifted to the Eastern front in the Second World War, where more people fought and died than in all other theatres of war around the world together.[15]

Murray offers another challenge to those who would use recent conflicts, such as the Gulf War (and by extension the recent 2003 war in Iraq), to predict that technology will dominate future warfare. He argues that we cannot really judge past RMAs let alone the present one because the historical record is not yet complete, and that until analysis based on detailed research is published, most contemporary commentaries may be misleading. Murray points out that it was not until the 1980s that historians began to unravel what actually took place on battlefields of 1914–18. This is precisely Biddle's contention when he asserts that many conclusions about the Gulf War drawn from early accounts lacked the data to support the conclusions. Biddle claims that only with the publication of works based on a more complete analysis of the data, which can take years to complete properly, can a reliable evaluation of the lessons of the war be conducted. For example, immediately after the Gulf War many saw it as the epitome of an RMA-based victory. Subsequent detailed studies of the US military's command and control shortcomings, however, found that serious deficiencies reduced the effectiveness of US forces and that some of them still exist today. The studies concluded that unless deficiencies in many areas are rectified, in the future the US may only be able to achieve success against "very weak, small opponents incapable of attacking the vulnerabilities" in the US system.[16] According to Murray, a close, evidence-based look at most case studies challenges the idea of a series of revolutions in military affairs, and he claims that the concept of RMAs distorts history and overlooks complex and ambiguous interactions among many factors.[17]

Stephen Biddle's iconoclastic interpretation of Coalition success in the Gulf War offers a model that incorporates both technology and human factors. His explanation of the Coalition victory posits a powerful synergistic interaction between a major skill imbalance and new technology to explain the outcome of the 1991 Gulf War. He theorizes that it was the extremely low skill level of Iraqi forces compared to Western forces in the Coalition plus the technical preponderance of the Coalition that allowed it to win a near bloodless victory. Biddle claims that higher Iraqi skill levels, even with the Iraqis' technological inferiority, would have resulted in significant Coalition casualties; likewise, lower Coalition skill levels, even with technological superiority, would also have resulted in significant Coalition casualties. His theory has important policy implications, because most current net assessment and force planning methodologies focus on numbers and the technical characteristics of adversaries' weapons. This methodology risks a serious misjudgement of the real military power of an opponent and could result in major errors in estimates in the forces needed to meet future threats. Arguments that modernization should be protected at the expense of training and readiness overestimate the value of technology and underestimate the role that skill in using technology has on the outcome of warfare, Biddle argues. He concludes that a more systematic study of opponents' skills is needed because little research has been done on the relationship between weapons effects and the skills of the operators on the outcome of battle.[18]

The real limits on exploiting the RMA may not be insufficient doctrine and technology, but, according to a view presented by the American National Defense Panel, the rigid and parochial military organizations that are unable to take full advantage of any potential RMA.[19] Szafranski takes up this argument and asserts that the shackles imposed by the current US defence appropriation process, an acquisition system based on competing separate services, and Combatant Comanders (formerly CINCs)[20] organized for operations in geographical areas will obstruct the required organizational changes. He concludes that the US armed services may dabble with new organizational forms, but that they are unlikely to change the system sufficiently to revolutionize their combat power. The US military, in his view, is as averse to change as it is to risk, and a true RMA requires changes in behaviours and attitudes that the US system is not capable of summoning forth. According to Szafranski, the US military cherishes evolutionary change, and that is what we should therefore expect to see.[21]

Others argue that today's military culture (with its saluting, uniforms, and drill) is largely a product of an industrial age army preoccupied by standardization, specialization, professionalization, synchronization, and centralization, and that structures which consist of officers and NCOs, still operating with the rank, deference, and pay structures of a bygone time, are not appropriate for future war.[22] A former chief of staff of the US Army, General Gordon Sullivan, contends that the information age is defined by less hierarchical learning organizations, with the network as the structure, not the pyramid, and knowledge, not equipment, as capital.[23] Others, reflecting van Creveld's ideas, suggest that the real RMA involves the increasing importance of support forces, constabulary functions in OOTW, and smaller forces with increases in transport, intelligence, communications, and psychological operations units.[24] In this scenario, information warriors might supplant "operators," like combat arms officers and pilots, as the source of new military leaders.[25] Taking this hypothesis a step further, if we accept Kasurak's conclusion that civilianization in the military is a "product of technology," then as technology affects all aspects of society and the military more profoundly, it may weaken the military's monopoly on "functionally relevant information." This could fragment the military profession into specialist subgroups oriented toward civilian technological functions. These subgroups – much like the technical subcultures we see in air forces – could become "alienated," leading to a decrease in internal cohesion in the military profession.[26]

HUMAN IMPLICATIONS OF THE REVOLUTION IN MILITARY AFFAIRS

Changes in military technology and organization, whether or not caused by an RMA, connote changes in the human dimension of armed forces. Patrick Mileham examines this issue and claims that "alongside the RMA there has been a revolution in the demands of moral sensibility required of leaders," a trend Milehan believes will continue in the future.[27] He provides a British perspective on motivation, corporate spirit, and leadership in future military operations, and he notes that the blurring of roles and tasks assigned to leaders today – "sending a message to Saddam" or bombing to enforce human rights – together with the face of the new battlefield will make the job of future leaders very difficult. Mileham raises the question of whether the "tolerance for ambiguity" often cited as a desirable characteristic for the highest levels of military and political leadership might not be seen as duplicity, in some cases, by those being led.[28] To deal with this issue, military forces need to add a clearly defined moral relationship to traditional interpretations of leadership. If the leader is competent, followed, and successful, there is no divergence between the other aspects of leadership and its moral component, but if the leader is seen to fail, that failure can diminish the strength of the moral component of his/her leadership. A clearly defined moral relationship is required to ensure that the "leader defines and personifies the moral responsibility for his own and others' actions and the consequences," Mileham argues.[29]

He goes on to say that all leaders, from the corporal to the Commander-in-Chief, will need to develop a new sort of moral toughness and a better intellectual grasp of the issues than in the past because the information and knowledge revolution is increasing our reliance on virtual reality exponentially, "which can cause moral divergence from reality."[30] The new synthetic world of cyberspace, where some parts of future wars will be fought, risks divorcing servicemen and women from the human aspects of war unless leaders reinforce the relationships between real space and cyberspace, based on moral character and knowledge. Mileham cautions us that front-line forces have yet to appreciate the moral considerations of future war much beyond rules of engagement. He warns us that we face a moral incomprehensibility similar to that which would have resulted from a nuclear exchange in the Cold War, but this time caused by the increasing use of mass information distributed by communications technology.[31]

Mileham also raises the issue of leadership and delegation in operations other than war. He contends that as these types of operations become the norm, the nature of leadership "is passing the leader-decision-making point rapidly around as well as up and down the chain of command." He points out that the military is accustomed to delegation in relatively static and linear forms and that empowerment "seems to be embedded in the technological components of fighting power." However, because most operations carry "high politico-ethical agendas" their conduct relies crucially on the moral component of every leader "down to the self-led." This implies that, in addition to the physical aspects of leadership, we now need "much more intuitive moral judgement at all levels." The expanding number of leaders and the level down to which important decisions are being delegated lends some credence to the suggestion that we may be coming close to an all-officer structure for the armed forces.[32]

In discussing the connection between discipline and self-discipline, Mileham believes that because of the delegation of leadership and the failure of written legal and ethical codes to keep up with military operations in the new world order, self-discipline is an important human resource required as a moral component of fighting power. But self-discipline is not inculcated by "formal" or traditional discipline, but by effective leaders who develop the self-discipline and moral maturity of their followers.

Mileham sees trust as the heart of military ethics, noting that the British Army's ethos statement emphasizes "mutual trust." However, if the onus for moral behaviour has cascaded down through the ranks, then it is not just in the commissioned officer ranks that we seek integrity. Mileham distinguishes between "character" (the deeply rooted predisposition for individuals to act morally) and "personality" (patterns of behaviour) to suggest that leaders have a responsibility to develop their followers' character and that organizations must seek persons of character. He concludes by suggesting that leaders in the future bear a more onerous responsibility than in the past, and to fulfill this responsibility they will need to link leadership even more closely to morality, self-discipline, and morale than has been done in the past.[33]

Oliver sees the RMA as an interesting "test case" for the evolving professionalism of the CF, as well as for the political conditions which permit professionalism to flourish. According to Oliver, the most important challenge posed by the RMA is intellectual, because "flexibility of thought and habit" will be needed to adapt to "rapid changes in weapons technology, communications, and delivery systems in the years to come, regardless of the particular systems and technologies involved." The technical and educational requirements of the RMA make it likely that "many future professionals will likely operate in a much broader middle ground between the old categories of civilian and military, thanks in part to what might be called knowledge proliferation, both horizontally and vertically." Oliver argues that the specialized expertise "so much a part of the profession of arms in the last two centuries and so indicative of professional, industrial-era armies, might now be breaking down," as mercenaries, contractors, and others are able to fulfill functions that were previously the exclusive domain of military officers.[34]

Bland's assessment of the future sees "no better times ahead for senior military leaders" because, in Canadian defence policy, even "new governments tend to follow old formulae." Bland argues that Canadian officers need to change their views about some of their fundamental assumptions underlying national defence and "bring them into line with mainstream Canadian political thinking." However, this will require "officers to reconsider the framework of ideas that has until now shaped their belief system." Bland challenges some of these assumptions in posing the following questions: "Is it reasonable in the circumstances to insist that the Canadian Forces should be capable of fighting a first-class enemy in a high-intensity combat environment and that no other model is appropriate to Canada's defence needs? Is it always in the national interests to harmonize Canadian plans, force structures, doctrine, rules of engagement, and other policies to fit the needs of allies? Should Canadian officers continue to embrace allies and look to their ideas and directions as models for the Canadian Forces?"

Bland provides some clues to the answers to these questions when he asserts that "military concepts and doctrine" cannot alter in any meaningful way "political ideas and attitudes concerning national defence." He therefore suggests that the officer corps will have to rethink its "assumptions about threats, defence objectives, capabilities, organizations, relations with allied military leaders, and operational methods" to bring their assumptions into line with the way most Canadians think about national defence.[35]

Oliver reminds us that in accommodating change the profession of arms has a right to reject some of the reforms suggested by various commissions and boards without being labelled unprofessional or "anti-intellectual." He offers us this vision of the military of the future: "Sir John Hackett and others have argued that the advent of the mass citizen army brought the civilian and military worlds into greater alignment, even as industrialization and military labour specialization drove them farther apart. We might now speculate that the post-modern profession of arms will borrow from both traditions: an elite, professional army of military specialists possessed of unique abilities and awesome capabilities, yet one tied closely to civil society by accountability, transparency, and personnel and technical dependence. It will be a small but fabulously well-trained cyber-citizenry-in-arms, both emboldened and ensnared by intimate connections with civil society."[36]

OPERATIONS OTHER THAN WAR

In the future, military forces are likely to be used frequently in "non-traditional" roles, sometimes described as operations other than war (OOTW). Traditionally, the US military has preferred to wage short, decisive wars in which American technical and material superiority is brought to bear to overwhelm the enemy.[37] Despite the fact that military success has been described as "the fundamental requirement of American strategic culture," decisive success has been hard to come by in post–Cold War operations.[38] In part because of this aspect of its strategic culture, there is evidence that the American public is not convinced that its military power should be committed for political purposes[39] in the same way that the Canadian public fully supports peacekeeping missions by the CF as a way of enhancing Canada's prestige on the world stage. For this reason, American military culture is founded on what some commentators see as the only proper role for the US armed forces: "Winning the nation's wars."[40]

For many in the armed forces of Canada and the US, preparing for conventional warfare like the two world wars and the Gulf War is their main raison d'être. But Bland points out that, horrific as they were, the two world wars of the twentieth century were anomalies. Since the histories of the world wars are so pervasive and strong in all media, however, they tend to obscure the more likely type of future military operations – OOTW. Nevertheless, the world wars raised the profile of military aspects of national policy and promoted the view that "if a state is prepared for global warfare, then it is effectively prepared for any conflict," a view which has prevailed in many military circles. Bland says that this is "a dangerous assumption" that has "unnecessarily dislocated national defence planning in many states."[41]

The counter-argument to Bland is that although OOTW are essential to the national interest of the Western states, they have a detrimental effect on combat readiness and cause uncertainty among soldiers about the essential combat focus of military forces. Even though some American units reported that OOTW provided solid training and good leadership experience for junior officers and NCOs, the retraining of units after peacekeeping operations to meet rigorous combat readiness standards was seen by some as an unacceptable drain on scarce resources.[42] Furthermore, studies have shown that the US Army is losing some of its best junior officers because they see it becoming an increasingly bureaucratic organization whose focus is dictated by peacekeeping missions.[43]

Canadian officers also argue that the CF's primary aim must be to fight and win wars, but they are more flexible in terms of acknowledging that this must not be the CF's only focus. They see the CF as anchored in a "war-fighting paradigm," but also capable of a whole range of missions in the OOTW spectrum. However, they caution that the CF must beware of an erosion in their military ethos if there is an inadequate focus on war fighting in the CF.[44]

The Canadian position that peacekeeping and combat skills are compatible with each other has been the subject of some debate.

The statement attributed to the late UN secretary-general Dag Hammerskjold – "Peacekeeping is not a mission for a soldier but only a soldier can do it"[45] – highlights the difficulties in resolving this issue. Despite some claims that peace support operations have become more accepted by the US armed forces as normal military tasks that require specific and intense training,[46] research conducted at the US Army War College in 1997–98 suggests that there is a disconnect in US Army doctrine and training that prepares troops to be combat-ready but does not prepare them adequately for OOTW, especially peacekeeping operations. While those surveyed expressed the view that combat capability would be degraded with increased peace support training, respondents acknowledged that there was an urgent need for such training if forces were going to be deployed on these types of missions.[47] These views turned out to be prophetic when the 3rd Battalion of the 504th Parachute Infantry Regiment of the 82nd Airborne Division in Kosovo in 1999 was involved in violations of military law, the prescribed rules of engagement, and even the army's "core values" of dignity, respect, and tolerance. The factors that contributed to these incidents are a matter of debate. Some have attributed them to assigning a peace support role to a combat unit that was not properly trained for it; others claim an "unhealthy command climate" within the battalion was responsible for these incidents.[48]

The most credible challenge to the traditional American military view that peace support missions degrade combat capability is found in data collected by Charles Moskos and Laura Miller on various peacekeeping operations and humanitarian missions in Somalia, Haiti, Bosnia, and Macedonia. The data show that soldiers did not perceive a deterioration in their combat skills, and, if anything, they actually improved as soldiers in these kinds of missions. Data collected by Miller in Somalia also revealed that, relatively speaking, American forces behaved much better toward the local population, not only compared to so-called Third World armies but also compared to most of the Western armies, for example those from Italy or Belgium or Canada. Moskos and Miller believe that one of the main factors accounting for the better behaviour of US soldiers was that the Americans were the only mixed gender and mixed race force in Somalia, and that the culture of this force developed certain kinds of peacekeeping proclivities which the other countries were not able to take advantage of.[49]

Of more concern than the effect of peace support missions on American military culture to some observers in the US is the recent trend, despite legal restrictions, to employ the American military in domestic (aid to civil power) activities, such as the war on drugs, maintaining civil order (e.g., the Los Angeles riots of 1992), patrolling the border with Mexico, and disaster relief.[50] If one accepts that the roles of military forces help to define their culture, then this would suggest that the American military may be moving away from its traditional war-fighting focus to a more varied outlook.

This debate is not likely to be resolved until more evidence is gathered on the differences between preparing armed forces for war and OOTW and the effects that training for OOTW may have on combat readiness. The consensus of Canadians, and others, involved in peace support operations is that the wide range of missions, from humanitarian aid to high intensity combat, requires combat-capable troops who have received specialized training. It has also been suggested that, in the future, it would be useful to reduce the perceived dichotomy some claim exists between "warriors" and "peacekeepers."[51]

In any event, if one accepts the argument that Canadian governments continue to use the CF as part of a foreign policy based on "pragmatic idealism," then one can accept that Canadian defence policy will continue along much the same lines as it has in the past. Canadian governments will use the armed forces as a way to maintain a place at the table in traditional alliances and it will also use them to participate in peacekeeping missions that are perceived to ensure international, and by extension Canadian, security.[52] In these circumstances, the Canadian officer corps bears the responsibility of preparing the CF to be ready to carry out the tasks the government gives them.

THE FUTURE OF CANADIAN CULTURE AND CANADIAN MILITARY CULTURE

Another key factor in understanding what the future holds for the culture of the CF's officer corps and the CF are the trends in the development of Canadian social values at the beginning of the twenty-first century. Some observers predict that globalization will result in a half-dozen or less international "megacultures" which will displace current national cultures. Others point to the resurgence of ethnic identities around the world to argue that distinctions between cultures may blur, but that the old cultures will not die easily. Still others suggest that the tension between individuals' desire for "roots" in a culture and some sort of universal culture based on globalization will not disappear.[53]

Economist William Watson's analysis of globalization and its meaning for Canada tends to accentuate the optimistic view about the survival of Canadian culture. Watson maintains that the whole world has caught "the Canadian disease" whose symptoms are fear of economic and cultural domination by the Americans. Despite globalization's seemingly pervasive homogenization of world culture, there is still room for Canadians to determine their own destiny as a nation. The greatest threat to Canada's continued existence, according to Watson, is the intermingling of cultures through new communications technologies.[54]

Watson goes on to say that Canadian nationalists' concept of a nation's culture rests heavily on the notion of "common Canadian cultural experiences." But he argues that the only time in our country's history that this common experience existed to any great degree was for a few years in the 1950s, before large antennas, cable, and satellite television, when CBC television had a "captive audience." This analysis ignores the effect of the print media and radio before television and the fact that even with television the two solitudes of French- and English-Canadian culture have endured. Watson does acknowledge that for most of our, and the world's, history human beings have not had common cultural experiences. Before the 1920s, which brought the widespread popularity of radio, most people's culture was influenced strongly by local events. Even so, Watson points out that common experience does not imply common understanding of the events, and that today, as throughout our history, there are deep divisions among the West, Central Canada, the Maritimes, and Quebec. Nevertheless, as Watson observes, we "are a community based on memory," even if that memory is "imperfect and conflicting."[55]

Watson's view is supported by Adams's analysis of twenty-five years of polling data by the Environics Research Group. It shows that Canadians "feel strongly about the right to live in a society that allows its citizens to be detached from ideology ... and not feel obliged to be jingoistic or sentimentally patriotic." Canada is also distinguished by its tolerance of diversity, and this correlates with support for "modern" trends such as gender equality, according to Adams. Most Canadians believe in a kinder, gentler social order as opposed to the dominant "survival of the fittest" ideology prevalent in the US. Adams concludes that the socio-cultural differences between the US and Canada may diminish over time but will remain significant for "many generations to come."[56]

Another factor that has a huge impact on Canadian culture is immigration, as the number of Canadians of neither British nor French origin has grown tremendously since the end of the Second World War. Even though since 1950 the immigrant population of Canada has been stable at about 16 per cent of the total population, the per centage of non-Europeans has changed dramatically. Between 1961 and 1971, 75 per cent of immigrants to Canada were from Europe or the US; in the decade 1981–91 that number dropped to 29 per cent while the proportion of immigrants from Asia, Africa, the Caribbean, and Latin America increased to 70 per cent. And Canada's immigrant population could increase by three million people by 2010. These figures indicate that theories of the international and multicultural dimensions of organizations, like Pheysey's, may be vital to understanding Canada's military culture in the future.[57]

Another key, future issue for the Canadian officer corps is the representation of visible minorities in the CF. In 1996, the 3.2 million people belonging to visible minorities living in Canada represented 11.2 per cent of the population.[58] In addition, "over 80 per cent of the visible minority population aged 15 and over are immigrants to Canada, not Canadian-born, and the majority of these have immigrated since the 1980s."[59] However, the majority of the applicants for the CF today (usually seventeen to twenty-four years old), are still mainly of British or French origin as they were twenty years ago. Yet even though the total number of "Aboriginal and visible minority applicants for the CF, when compared to the total population, was consistent with their representation in society," data from the mid-1990s "shows that the visible minority and Aboriginal acceptance into the CF is nearly one-third lower than for the rest of society."[60] A similar situation exists with women and the CF. The CF are receiving more women applicants than ever before, with 20 per cent of its applicants now female, but women have not been very successful at surviving the initial stages of recruiting and training, because, as we have seen, women comprise only about 11 per cent of the CF. In short, the socio-demographic composition of the CF applicant pool tends to be relatively narrow, consisting mainly of young, urbanized, secondary school educated males with British or French backgrounds. Other ethnic groups are significantly under-represented. One reason for this is that to many new Canadians – who may come from societies where the military is associated with repression – the CF are an unknown, if not an alien force.[61]

If it is to maintain its diversity targets in the future, the CF will have to attract and retain more recruits from visible minority groups. This may cause difficulties with current basic-training programs as the socialization process, with its emphasis on the assimilation rather than the integration of recruits, does not adequately take into account the differences newcomers bring into the military. Castonguay claims that this process may well be difficult to change because too many "leaders still operate with dated mindsets of the world" and do not fully appreciate the changes that have occurred in national cultures, the nature of work, and the nature of people in the organization. If officers, as leaders in the organization, are responsible for guiding change in the organizational culture, then they must have "a broad knowledge of history, culture, technology and human relations." To ensure that newcomers are integrated effectively into the CF, especially into their initial units, leaders need more than just knowledge of the military aspects of their profession. They must also understand human behaviour and be prepared to prevent or resolve conflicts and to develop and motivate cohesive groups whose members are more diverse than in the past. Based on this analysis, Castonguay concludes that it is possible that not all officers in the CF will be capable of commanding pluralistic units in the future.[62]

On the other hand, some senior Canadian army officers do not see any contradiction between good order and discipline in a modern army and civil rights. It is a question of good leadership: "We are dealing with people who have decided to join the army ... Our job is to instil self-discipline in them ... to get the soldiers to follow the rules because they believe in them." From this standpoint, the "crisis of leadership" in the 1990s is attributed to a "crisis of values, not of ability."[63]

Getting young Canadians to join the CF in the future may be problematic as studies have shown that they, more than any other generation before them, have "abandoned fear, guilt, and duty as major motivating factors."[64] A recent Environics Research Group survey found that 62 per cent of young civilians of military age in Canada were "opposed to war under any circumstances," and a 1997 study done by Environics for DND showed that only 24 per cent of "civilians who expressed an interest in joining the regular force were motivated by the vocational ideal of service to others." The majority were motivated by the occupational ideals of job security, education, pay, or exciting work.[65] These findings are similar to those in the military sociology literature which depicts "postmodern" military forces as those whose soldiers are increasingly motivated more by "the desire to have a meaningful personal experience than out of either national patriotism or an occupational incentive." The fact that Canada has moved "earliest and farthest from the traditional model" of military culture has been attributed to the high value that the CF places on integrating military values with the values of Canadian society, leading to the CF itself becoming, like its parent society, more "democratized, liberalized, and civilianized."[66]

In spite of these indicators of differences between the Canadian and US armed forces, there are some risks that certain parts of the Canadian officer corps may become "Americanized." The tendency of the three environmental components of the CF, but particularly the air force and the navy, to prefer combined operations with their US counterparts to joint operations with the other CF environmental components is a persistent pressure toward Americanization. Certain officers in the Canadian Air Force, and Navy to a lesser extent, spend a large portion of their careers on exchange positions with the US forces. In rare cases, long term exposure to the US military culture may result in a high degree of Americanization. I have been acquainted with some CF officers who spent over half their careers in the US, in some cases marrying American nationals, and thereby adopted many values, attitudes, and beliefs common to the US armed forces. While the number of these officers is probably quite small, it does illustrate what could happen if circumstances were to change for the CF as a whole. However, as long as Canada maintains its own military institutions – like RMC and the Canadian Forces College – that are capable of transmitting Canadian military culture to each successive generation of officers, this culture will probably continue to survive and evolve as a distinct entity. Some believe that these institutions have not been capable of inculcating a strong, unified Canadian military culture,[67] but until more empirical research is conducted on this subject it will continue to be a moot point. What is more certain, as a recent DND report on strategic human resource issues has pointed out, is that unless the CF are able to provide a career to young Canadians based on a profession with its own military ethos but which is also compatible with Canadian values, the CF will have difficulty attracting and retaining the high calibre young people it needs.[68] In the end the question of Americanization may be determined by Canadian society at large. The most recent polls support the historic, paradoxical nature of Canadian perceptions of the issue as about 50 per cent of those surveyed believed that "Canadians are more like Americans,"[69] but 90 per cent thought that "we are a distinct society."[70]

MILITARY CULTURE AND THE FUTURE

The future of war may be impossible to predict, as an examination of the predictions made before the two world wars about the coming wars and the doctrine of the major belligerents in 1914 and 1939 shows that there was a wide divergence of views but no consensus about the future. Virtually every possibility was explored in the literature and the press, but it was impossible to know, before the fighting started, which prediction would be most accurate. Perhaps Michael Howard's comment on doctrine best sums up the situation: "I am tempted to declare dogmatically that whatever doctrine the Armed Forces are working on now, they have got it wrong. I am also tempted to declare that it does not matter that they have got it wrong. What does matter is their capacity to get it right quickly when the moment arrives."[71] If Howard's analysis is correct, success in future wars or OOTW will be determined by the military force's culture, and to a lesser extent by its doctrine. What type of culture, then, should the Canadian and American forces of the future have in order to deal with the unpredictability of future war?

The CSIS report suggests that the dominant force to reshape US military culture in the future may be the breathtaking advances in communications and information technology we are experiencing. Despite these changes, war will remain a constant. Therefore, military culture will set the conditions of success in future peace and war as much as technology will. To successfully cope with war and OOTW in the future, military culture must encompass core military values as a counterweight to the innate conservatism of military hierarchies and the inertia of large defence bureaucracies. Unfortunately, according to the CSIS report, many current military leaders were raised in an era of relative information scarcity, and this leaves them "singularly unprepared to deal with today's usual problems of information overload." A culture of top-down micromanagement, which is not only dysfunctional for adaptive organizations but also runs contrary to most Western military doctrine, has resulted.[72] An effective military culture for the twenty-first century, the CSIS study argues, must be different from the one that exists in the US. It should incorporate "new patterns of leadership; more agile, streamlined organizations; redefinitions of the civil-military relationship; and renewed attention to the ethics of modern warfare."[73]

Changing military culture to achieve these aims will not be easy. Highly successful business organizations, while maintaining core values, are willing to discard policies that are deemed to be unsuccessful at reinforcing those values. They also do not hesitate to change senior leadership, often bringing in outsiders to the organization to effect policy change. In contrast, military organizations rarely bring in new leadership to change organizational policies and values, and this limits the organizations' ability to effect significant change. The CF's experiences with "civilianization" have brought some new leadership into the Canadian defence organization, but the results have not been uniformly positive, as we have seen, especially in terms of preserving military over business values.

According to Bell, successful organizations have three learning-related characteristics: (1) well-developed core values and competencies, (2) an attitude that supports continuous improvement, and (3) the ability to fundamentally renew or revitalize themselves. Bell claims, however, that the US Army in particular is likely to resist real change, because much of its senior leadership denies that any serious problems exist and it believes that its army culture has become "an immutable entity." Both Bell and the CSIS report argue that the only effective way to ensure that the American officer corps has the core values it requires to lead effectively in the future is to create an external panel or task force to provide the oversight and institutional stamina needed to help force change and to provide feedback on the policies, values, and culture of the American military.[74] The post-Somalia CF experience, however – with various monitoring committees, boards, and commissions of inquiry, plus the appointment of a CF ombudsman – shows that, as Bell implies, unless change is co-ordinated and driven forcefully from the top down, little of enduring worth will be accomplished.[75]

The future is filled with challenges for the armed services of Canada and the US. The key to meeting these challenges will be the ability of the services to cope with unpredictable change. At the moment, it is not clear that they are ready to cope with this change. However, of the two nations, being smaller, unified, and more open to the winds of social change, the armed forces of Canada may be in a better position than the American services to weather the storms of the future, and at the same time provide a model for its larger allies to emulate.

8

Conclusions

Answering the questions posed at the beginning of this book is not an easy task. The issues of how such phenomena as the Revolution in Military Affairs, coalition operations, and the push toward interoperability with the US will affect the uniqueness of Canadian military doctrine and philosophy; whether it is inevitable that American military values and ethics will be absorbed and internalized by Canadian officers; or whether the Canadian officer corps is at risk of being "Americanized" are complex and inter-related. The approach taken here has been to use the concept of culture, the "bedrock of military effectiveness,"[1] in an attempt to find some answers to these questions. Culture here is used to help explain the "motivations, aspirations, norms and rules of conduct," what might be called the essence, of the Canadian and American military cultures.[2] This perspective also allows us to understand how new technologies may influence and in turn be influenced by military culture in the future.

The literature on military culture has grown rapidly over the past five years, but there is little common focus in the writings that have appeared in diverse publications. Representative theoretical constructs from the field of organizational behaviour have been used here to examine military culture in Canada and the US because the field's multidisciplinary approach allows inquiry on a broad front. It is acknowledged that there are different ways of interpreting and studying culture in the disciplines that contribute to the organizational behaviour literature, but three major interpretations (by Schein, Sorensen and Pedersen, and Pheysey) were used here to show how each has applications to the study of military culture. A key concept in the organizational behaviour literature is that of adaptive versus non-adaptive cultures. This concept has been applied in the analysis of Canadian and American military culture, and it has been shown that both these cultures exhibit characteristics of non-adaptive cultures, including resistance to change.

The profession of arms is another key concept in the book because this concept embodies the virtues and ethical norms that the military professionals, who are those with the legal and moral responsibility for deciding what aspects of military culture need to be changed and then effecting that change, should possess. While the officer corps has generally been identified as the group that should determine, shape, and reinforce the culture of military organizations, in the CF, non-commissioned members of the force are frequently portrayed as the guardians of the organization's culture, at least for the other ranks. Therefore, the role of NCMs in the evolution of Canadian military culture appears to be an area where research is required. As we have seen, one of the greatest challenges for the profession of arms in the twenty-first century will be to redefine itself to meet the needs of a society that appears to be increasingly indifferent to the demands of a vocation or calling. From this it follows that the greatest challenge for military leaders today is to decide which parts of military culture should be kept and which parts should be discarded or modified for armed services to remain relevant to the societies they serve.

However, Canadian military leaders face a particular challenge in effecting organizational change. In the past, the Canadian officer corps was not particularly well educated or well prepared to lead change. The criticism in commentaries on various "crises" in Canadian military ethos and leadership in the past forty years lend credence to this viewpoint. There is evidence in recent changes to Canadian professional military education that some of these faults are being addressed. But no matter how well-prepared officers are to lead change, without evidence and data to answer basic questions about the nature of Canadian military culture, they are unlikely to be able to make informed decisions about what needs to be changed and what needs to remain unchanged in a future Canadian military culture. Until serious scholarship is able to start to answer these questions, the outlook for effective change in the CF leading up to 2020 and beyond is bleak. A number of research areas offer promise to help address these issues.

The organizational behaviour literature demonstrates that national cultures have a strong influence on organizational cultures; the Canadian and American armed services can thus be expected to be products of the societies from which they are drawn. Conversely, armed forces have been used throughout history to effect change in civil society. Recent statements published by DND have indicated that the government of Canada believes that it is appropriate for the CF to implement certain policies designed to influence Canadian civil culture. The historical analogies referred to in this study offer some insights into how other nations have used their armed forces to effect social change. While there are no exact historical parallels to the Canadian situation, comparative cultural research might be useful in this area.

The ethos of an armed force has a significant effect on its culture and way of doing things. A hotly debated topic in the US today is the gap that is desirable or permissible between the military and the civilian ethos in a nation. In Canada this debate has focused largely on the degree of "civilianization" in the Canadian military and whether this is good or bad. The general consensus among most writers is that too many civilian values have been assimilated by the CF, and that these values are debasing the fundamental war-fighting ethos of the CF. Pedersen and Sorensen's model of an organization dominated by differentiation, inconsistency, ambiguity, and conflict, instead of a paramount, cohesive culture, appears to fit the CF. Some empirical data has been collected over the last thirty years on these subjects, but no comprehensive study of the Canadian military ethos and its relation to Canadian military culture has yet to be conducted.

The US armed services have problems similar to the CF's, according to recent studies. Morale and readiness have suffered because of flaws in their organizational climate and possibly their organizational culture. The officer corps, especially the senior leadership of the American military, has been singled out for most of the blame because, through promotion and other officer development policies, it has pursued a careerist agenda that places self above service, reversing the traditional, espoused US military ethos. Dissonance between espoused values and actual values-in-use in the US military has resulted in a crisis of confidence between subordinates and superiors, especially senior leaders. There is evidence that the US military exhibits some of the characteristics of a dysfunctional cultural paradigm which has generated a non-adaptive culture that is characterized by cautious leaders who try to protect their own interests by behaving insularly, politically, and bureaucratically. New members of the organization are quickly socialized to these realities of the cultural paradigm, and those who have prospered have been those who have adopted the values-in-use. This does not bode well for dynamic reform in the American military, as these leaders have been characterized as resisting meaningful change to a system they have grown attached to over time. Therefore, there seems to be little hope that the institutional momentum necessary to force significant change in the US armed services will be generated in the foreseeable future. The parallels with Canadian circumstances might provide clues to how the CF can address similar problems.

The nature and meaning of the gap between the cultures of the American military and civilian society are the subject of a debate with extremes of opinion. The most comprehensive study of the subject, the Triangle Institute for Security Studies project, concluded that concerns about the civil-military gap in the US are justified but should not be exaggerated. Some literature on Canadian civil-military relations exists, but very little empirical evidence has been produced to address how the civil-military gap in Canada might affect Canadian military culture. The large body of American research on the civil-military gap, as Okros has indicated, may not apply to the Canadian case because of cultural differences between the two countries.

A new Canadian military culture could be said to have been created with the unification of the CF in 1968. It is epitomized at NDHQ, where bureaucratization and civilianization have spawned a new culture built on business practices and efficiency rather than the virtues of the traditional warrior ethos often espoused by the military. Officers, particularly senior officers, who spend a significant part of their careers in the national capital, are perceived as being more interested in their careers than in service to the nation. The result has been a conflict between espoused values and values-in-use in the CF, a lack of trust between superiors and subordinates, and some of the characteristics of a non-adaptive culture identified in the US military today. However, because the causes of these features of CF culture are different from the causes of problems in the US armed services' culture, their manifestation also appears to be different from the American pattern. Although the nature of Canadian military culture today is another fruitful area for research, some tentative conclusions can be stated based on the analysis conducted in this study.

While there are differences between the Canadian and American military cultures, there is no doubt that the CF have been Americanized to some extent. As long as DND and the CF pursue a deliberate policy of fostering interoperability with US forces, adopting US doctrine, and applying American RMA-based technical solutions to Canadian defence problems, the CF will certainly continue to incorporate American ways of thinking about military operations and aspects of American military culture will continue to permeate the Canadian officer corps. These trends toward Amercanization will be reinforced by our geographic proximity and cultural similarity to our neighbours to the south. However, the evidence also suggests that while the Canadian officer corps has certainly become more Americanized since the Second World War, it is in no imminent danger of losing its identity. One of the key factors for maintaining a distinct military culture is having distinct roles as a military force. As long as the CF continue to have roles that are clearly different from the US military, it is likely that the CF will maintain a separate military culture. The other key factors to maintaining the CF's cultural autonomy are the "invariants" of geography, historical experience, political alliances, and national culture. In many ways they draw us toward the US, but in other ways, as we have seen, they separate us from the American republic.

Almost thirty years ago, R.B. Byers and Colin Gray noted that the search for a distinctive Canadian military ethos paralleled the search for identity in other areas of Canadian life.[3] It appears that such an identity exists, but that there is often great difficulty in articulating it. Nevertheless, adopting increasingly American ways of doing things has found official sanction in DND policy. This has been reinforced by the desire of each of the three environmental components of the CF, especially of the air force and the navy, to work closely with their US counterparts. However, the idea that the CF's officer corps is being Americanized by being forced to accept a foreign doctrine and philosophy has its mythical aspects. As long as Canada has a separate national culture and its armed forces have distinct roles and institutions to transmit their culture, a unique Canadian military culture will endure.

In certain ways, the US military may be going down a path that the CF have already trodden. There is evidence that American military culture is being transformed in a fashion that could lead to the US forces becoming Canadianized. As they have been downsized, professionalized, and made subject to more civilian control, American forces have exhibited some of the characteristics of their Canadian cousins. Furthermore, as the roles of the US armed services have changed to approach more closely those performed by the CF in the last fifty years, there has been an influence on American military culture which could be described as Canadianization. This may be the path the US armed services will follow in the future.

Despite all the attention paid to technology in current discussions revolving around the RMA, we know that how humans select and use technology has a great deal to do with their cultural preferences. The military is a prime example of this tenet. History has shown that it is not technology itself, but how technology has been perceived and used, as guided by doctrine, that has spelled success or failure for armed forces in the past. However, to be successful doctrine must be capable of being adapted to change. But doctrine is determined by culture as much as anything else, and so for doctrine to be useful it must reside in a military culture that can cope with change effectively. One of the greatest potential problems in the CF today is the fascination that some of its members have with the RMA. Those in Canada who unabashedly embrace the technological aspects of the RMA seem unaware that many of its underlying assumptions are culturally-based and designed to serve an American audience. Until a more balanced approach is taken to the RMA in this country's defence establishment, the CF, in the name of interoperability, are likely to be saddled with expensive technology that does not meet their needs. The whole issue of the RMA's applicability to Canada should be carefully examined from the perspective of military culture so that those technologies that are compatible with the Canadian military culture can be acquired in a timely fashion and those that are not can be avoided.

A number of behavioural scientists have argued that Canada has moved "earliest and farthest from the traditional model" of military culture because of the high value that the CF places on integrating military values with the values of Canadian society and because of the attributes of democratization, liberalization, and civilianization found in Canadian military culture.[4] Other writers hypothesize that Canada may represent "the more contemporary or even the future form of military life."[5] Given the strengths and weaknesses in Canadian military culture, it is difficult to know if this is a good or a bad thing, but we clearly need to understand this issue more fully before any conclusive judgment can be passed. Unfortunately, much of the literature on military culture relies on a theoretical approach that may be too narrow, especially in the Canadian context.

The work of Schein is the theoretical foundation for much of the debate on military culture in the US. His link between strong cultures and both organizational effectiveness and the role leaders play in shaping culture has a natural appeal to Western armed forces. It reinforces their tendency to believe that robust, cohesive cultures are good and that military leaders have the most influence in shaping these cultures. However, the perspective provided by Sorensen and Pedersen may more accurately reflect organizational reality in North American armed forces. Differences among the army, navy, and air force, not to mention civilian defence employees, support Sorensen and Pedersen's concept of diverse and sometimes contradictory subcultures coexisting within armed services, leading to ambiguity and conflict in the cultures of the armed forces of Canada and the US. A further complication to the model provided by Schein is the increasing ethnic diversity that will be found in the Canadian and American armed forces in the future. Theories that address the performance of multicultural organizations, like Pheysey's, promise to be increasingly useful as our armed forces become more ethnically diverse. The implications for those studying Canadian military culture are that the American paradigm, largely based on Schein's theories of organizational culture, has its limitations. Future studies in Canadian military culture should, therefore, take into account other theories of organizational culture to better understand the Canadian situation.

From a practical perspective, the greatest impetus for the adoption of foreign doctrine and philosophy in the CF and Americanization in the CF's officer corps would appear to be the desire for interoperability by each of the three environmental components of the CF with their American counterparts rather than the impetus of any overarching American joint vision. Therefore, the CF need to approach issues of interoperability and co-operation with US forces carefully. American doctrine and the US forces' way of doing things reflect the nature of the US military culture. To adopt these practices unreservedly in the name of interoperability is fraught with risks. While there is no doubt that the CF must remain interoperable with their closest neighbour's armed forces, they should be aware that not all American practices will work in a Canadian military context. Rather than copy American doctrine almost word for word, as has been the practice in many cases in the past, the CF must ensure that procedures adopted in the name of interoperability will work in a Canadian military culture.

As a smaller, more agile and flexible organization, the CF are better positioned than their American allies to deal with change. The CF should resist the temptation, advocated by some, to become a virtual doctrinal clone of the US services and they should lead the way with innovative solutions to future challenges based on an adaptive Canadian military culture that has proved its worth in the past. But a clear understanding of where Canadian military culture stands today is needed before future courses can be charted. Delay only invites a repeat of some of the failures of the past. There is much to be done, and the sooner work begins, the better.

Notes

CHAPTER ONE

1 Granatstein, "American Influence on the Canadian Military," 132, 134, 137.

2 DND, "Shaping the Future of the Canadian Forces," 4, 8, 10. *Joint* is defined as activities, operations, organizations, etc., in which elements of more than one service of the same nation participate. *Combined* means activities, operations, organizations, etc., between two or more forces or agencies of two or more allies. ("Glossary," DND, *Canadian Forces Operations*.)

3 Adrian Preston, "Profession of Arms in Postwar Canada," 194, 203, 211.

4 Ulmer et al., *American Military Culture*, xv.

5 Johnston, "Doctrine Is Not Enough," 30.

6 Corum, "Clash of Military Cultures."

7 Johnston, "Doctrine is not Enough," 35.

8 Burk's definition is from Snider, "Uninformed Debate on Military Culture," 15–19.

9 Snider, "Uninformed Debate on Military Culture," 12, 14–15, 19.

10 Capstick, "Defining the Culture," 2.

CHAPTER TWO

1 Ulmer et al., *American Military Culture*, xv.

2 Castonguay, "Distinguish to Unite," 94–5.

3 Schermerhorn et al., *Organizational Behavior*, 57.

4 Most of this information on values is taken from standard organizational behaviour texts, including Schermerhorn et al., *Organizational Behavior*, 57–63; and Johns, *Organizational Behavior*, 114–27.
5 Schermerhorn et al., *Organizational Behavior*, 59.
6 Johns, *Organizational Behavior*, 117–18.
7 Ibid., 116.
8 Ibid., 116–17; and Schermerhorn et al., *Organizational Behavior*, 60.
9 Johns, *Organizational Behavior*, 119–20.
10 Ibid., 119–20.
11 Ibid., 120–1.
12 This is based on the theory of cognitive dissonance which predicts that inconsistency between a person's expressed attitude and his/her actual behaviour will result in changes in attitude, changes in behaviour, or new ways of rationalizing the inconsistency. (Schermerhorn et al., *Organizational Behavior*, 61.)
13 Johns, *Organizational Behavior*, 121–7.
14 Schermerhorn et al., *Organizational Behavior*, 60.
15 DND, Special Review Group, "Detailed Report of the Special Review Group-Operation Harmony (Rotation Two)."
16 Martin, *Cultures in Organizations*, v, 4, 13, 169.
17 Castonguay, "Distinguish to Unite," 94.
18 Martin, *Cultures in Organizations*, 4; and Pedersen and Sorensen, *Organisational Cultures in Theory and Practice*, 3.
19 Nelson and Quick, *Organizational Behavior*, 532.
20 Pedersen and Sorensen, *Organisational Cultures in Theory and Practice*, 1.
21 Pheysey, *Organizational Cultures*, 1, 2.
22 Pedersen and Sorensen, *Organisational Cultures in Theory and Practice*, 2.
23 Schein, *Organizational Culture and Leadership*, 15.
24 Pheysey, *Organizational Cultures*, 1, 2.
25 Robbins and Langton, *Organizational Behaviour*, 614.
26 Pedersen and Sorensen, *Organisational Cultures in Theory and Practice*, xiii.
27 Nelson and Quick, *Organizational Behavior*, 539.
28 Pedersen and Sorensen, *Organisational Cultures in Theory and Practice*, xiv.
29 Schein, *Organizational Culture and Leadership*, xii–xiii, xiv, 392.
30 Ibid., xv, 1–2, 5, 15, 227, 331–2.
31 Ibid., 12.
32 Ibid., 12–14.
33 Johnston, "Doctrine Is Not Enough," 35.

34 Nelson and Quick, *Organizational Behavior*, 536.
35 Pedersen and Sorensen, *Organisational Cultures in Theory and Practice*, 20.
36 Pheysey, *Organizational Cultures*, 4.
37 Nelson and Quick, *Organizational Behavior*, 537.
38 Schein, *Organizational Culture and Leadership*, 21–2, 25–6.
39 Ibid., 17–22, 25–6, 47.
40 Pedersen and Sorensen, *Organisational Cultures in Theory and Practice*, 7–8.
41 Arthur T. Hadley, *The Straw Giant*, 67–71.
42 Pedersen and Sorensen, *Organisational Cultures in Theory and Practice*, 20–2, 30.
43 Ibid., 8, 17, 116–18.
44 Nelson and Quick, *Organizational Behavior*, 542–4, 553.
45 *Power distance* is defined as "the willingness of a culture to accept status and power differences among its members. It reflects the degree to which people are likely to respect hierarchy and rank in organizations." (Schermerhorn et al., *Organizational Behavior*, 28.) In high power distance societies, people show a great deal of respect for those in authority and titles, status, and rank are very important. In low power distance societies, superiors still have authority but differences in rank and status are not accentuated. (Robbins, *Organizational Behaviour*, 5th ed., 66–7.)
46 Nelson and Quick, *Organizational Behavior*, 533–6.
47 Ibid., 547. See also Robbins and Langton, *Organizational Behaviour*, 625–39.
48 Castonguay, "Distinguish to Unite," 113.
49 Nelson and Quick, *Organizational Behavior*, 549.
50 Ibid., 549–51, 553.
51 Pheysey, *Organizational Cultures*, xiii, 3.
52 Schmitt, "Command and (Out of) Control," 55–8. See also Reimer, "Dominant Maneuver and Precision Engagement."
53 Pheysey, *Organizational Cultures*, 3.
54 Chris Wattie, "Absent-minded Professor Didn't Expect a Nobel," *Kingston Whig-Standard*, 13 October 1994, 9.
55 Pheysey, *Organizational Cultures*, 4–6.
56 Ibid., 7–8, 15–18.
57 Ibid., 94–5.
58 *Control*, in this context, is defined as "purposefully to direct or restrain the action of a force or thing." Ibid., 22.

59 Czerwinski, "Command and Control at the Crossroads," 121–32.
60 The origin of "office holders" in civilian organizations today comes from the *officiers* (office-holders) appointed by Charles VII at the end of the fifteenth century to command his army. Officers eventually evolved into military professionals. (John A. English, *Marching Through Chaos*, 3, 13.)
61 Pheysey, *Organizational Cultures*, 22–6.
62 Ibid., 26–7.
63 See Rothenberg, "Moltke, Schlieffen, and the Doctrine of Strategic Envelopment," 296, for the origins of *Auftragstaktik*.
64 Pheysey, *Organizational Cultures*, 26.
65 Berridge-Sills, "Computers and Strategy," 188.
66 Pheysey, *Organizational Cultures*, 32.
67 Ibid., 87–9, 93.
68 Bell, "Impact of Policies on Organizational Values and Culture," 6, 7, 11, 15n20, 16n30.
69 Ulmer et al., *American Military Culture*, xviii.
70 Snider, "Uninformed Debate on Military Culture," 14.
71 Nelson and Quick, *Organizational Behavior*, 539.
72 Robbins and Langton, *Organizational Behaviour*, 619, 623.
73 Nelson and Quick, *Organizational Behavior*, 540–1.
74 Ulmer et al., *American Military Culture*, xxv.
75 Bercuson, *Significant Incident*, 32–3.
76 Shy, "Jomini," 160.
77 Barzun, "Professions Under Siege," 124–5, 128, 130, 132.
78 Lerner, "Shame of the Professions," 138.
79 Huntington, "Officership as a Profession," 23–34. The theoretical concepts in this book are based on Huntington's essay.
80 See Baril, "Keynote Address." For critiques of Huntington see Burk, "Expertise, Jurisdiction, and Legitimacy of the Military Profession"; Feaver, "Civil-Military Problematique"; and Coffman, "Long Shadow of *The Soldier and the State*."
81 Bercuson, *Significant Incident*, 34, 36.
82 Commission of Inquiry into the Deployment of Canadian Forces to Somalia, *Dishonoured Legacy*, vol. 1, 81–2.
83 Edmonds, *Armed Services and Society*, 81, 84–5.
84 Commission of Inquiry into the Deployment of Canadian Forces to Somalia, *Dishonoured Legacy*, vol. 1, 80, 83.
85 Bland, "Canada's Officer Corps."

86 Commission of Inquiry into the Deployment of Canadian Forces to Somalia, *Dishonoured Legacy*, "Executive Summary," 50.
87 Oliver, "Canadian Military Professional Development."
88 Bercuson, *Significant Incident*, 37.
89 Breslin, "Organizational Culture and the Military," 12.
90 Bercuson, *Significant Incident*, 37.
91 Ibid., 35, 62–3.
92 Snider, "Uninformed Debate on Military Culture," 24–5.
93 Bercuson, *Significant Incident*, 108–9.
94 Bachman et al., "Distinctive Attitudes among US Enlistees," 577.
95 Bercuson, *Significant Incident*, 108–9.
96 Minister's Monitoring Committee on Change in the Department of National Defence and the Canadian Forces, "Second Interim Report of the Minister's Monitoring Committee on Change," chapter 5, "Observations."

CHAPTER THREE

1 Bercuson, *Significant Incident*, 27.
2 Soeters and Recht, "Culture and Discipline in Military Academies," 179,183.
3 Ibid., 171, 172, 175, 179.
4 Ibid., 172, 179, 183–4.
5 Described in Snider, "Uninformed Debate on Military Culture," 15–19.
6 Bercuson, *Significant Incident*, 41.
7 Sophie Perrier, "L'armée belge recrute hors de ses frontières." *Libération*, 8 Novembre 2000.
8 Edmonds, *Armed Services and Society*, 7, 12.
9 Skelton, "Samuel P. Huntington and the Roots of the American Military Tradition," 325–9.
10 Edmonds, *Armed Services and Society*, 14–16.
11 Builder, *Masks of War*, 3.
12 Edmonds, *Armed Services and Society*, 1–5, 8–18.
13 Rappaport in Edmonds, *Armed Services and Society*, 82–3.
14 Welch and Smith in Edmonds, *Armed Services and Society*, 90–1.
15 See Gilbert, "Machiavelli," 11–31 for a detailed explanation of Machiavelli's views.
16 John A. English, *Marching Through Chaos*, 13. See pp. 29–48 for a detailed description of this process.

17 Ben-Eliezer, *Making of Israeli Militarism*, 200.
18 Ibid., 195–7, 199–201.
19 Ibid. 215–16.
20 Ibid., 222–3.
21 Ibid., 226–7.
22 Michael Smith, "Might of the Military Cracks Under Pressure," *Telegraph*, 14 October 2000.
23 Korb, "Military and Social Change."
24 Edmonds, *Armed Services and Society*, 2, 5–6.
25 Ibid., 79–80.
26 Hillen, "Must US Military Culture Reform?" 9–23.
27 Sarkesian et al., *Soldiers, Society and National Security*, 140–2.
28 Owens, "Military Ethos and 'Don't Ask, Don't Tell.'"
29 Andre, "National Culture and Warfare," 108.
30 Hunt and Haycock, *Canada's Defence*, 1.
31 Loomis and Lightburn, "Taking into Account the Distinctness," 19–20.
32 Broadbent, "Military Society, Change or Decay, Part 1 & 2," part 1, 25; part 2, 30.
33 Owens, "Military Ethos and 'Don't Ask, Don't Tell.'"
34 Ferrill, "Elite Forces in the Ancient World,"41. See Ferrill, 38–41, for more detail on the Theban Sacred Band.
35 Owens, "Military Ethos and 'Don't Ask, Don't Tell.'"
36 John Moore, "Renewing DND's Culture: Lessons for the Way Ahead," 10–12. See this article for an example of the business approach to shape DND's behavioural norms.
37 Kasurak, "Civilianization and the Military Ethos," 109–10.
38 Ibid., 121.
39 Ibid., 109–10.
40 Ibid., 114, 116, 122, 128–9.
41 Critchley, "Civilianization and the Canadian Military," 226–37.
42 Ibid., 237–9.
43 Bland, "The Government of Canada and the Armed Forces," 27.
44 Ibid., 35.
45 Ibid., 39.
46 Ibid., 27.
47 Ibid., 31.
48 Ibid., 33–4.
49 Ibid., 35.
50 Ibid., 35–6.

51 Ibid., 39.
52 Ibid., 40–1.
53 Cited in Bland, "Canada's Officer Corps."
54 Ibid.
55 DND, "Shaping the Future of the Canadian Forces," 2–3.
56 Charles Cotton, personal communication to author, 12 January 2001; and Floyd Rudmin, "Acculturation and the Army" (presentation given at the Royal Military College of Canada, 19 January 2001).
57 DND, "Canada's Army," 34–5.
58 Breslin, "Organizational Culture and the Military," 14.
59 John A. English, *Marching through Chaos*, 4.
60 Keegan, *History of Warfare*, 75, 79–84.
61 Ibid., 85, 87–9, 103.
62 Ibid., 94–5, 98–9, 101.
63 Ibid., 108–10, 113–14.
64 See John A. English, *Marching Through Chaos*, 29–33 for details.
65 O'Connell, *Of Arms and Men*, 14–17, 24, 27–8.
66 Ibid., 30. See also Keegan, *History of Warfare*, 126–36.
67 Grant, "Closing the Doctrine Gap," 48–52.
68 O'Connell, *Of Arms and Men*, 53 (quotation), 36–8, 45–6, 51–8. O'Connell notes that long before the Greeks, Sumerian warriors (in 2,500 BC) used a full-fledged phalanx as their primary fighting formation because Sumerian warriors had a stake in their society, similar to the citizen soldiers in the ancient Greek city-states.
69 John A. English, *Marching Through Chaos*, 3, 13.
70 Keegan, *History of Warfare*, 177–81.
71 "Business has a Corrosive Effect on any Military Organisation," *Defence System Daily*, 7 September 1999. http://defence_data.com/current/page5191.htm
72 Rajiv Chandrasekaran, "Indonesian Military Wages Battle of Wills," *Washington Post Online*, 5 November 2000.

CHAPTER FOUR

1 Ulmer et al., *American Military Culture*, xvi, xix.
2 Robert Suro, "Pay, Morale Problems Still Beset Military," *Washington Post*, 10 January 2000.
3 Andre, "National Culture and Warfare," 108. Albert Legault's point that the US military has been more successful in recruiting minority

groups may be partially explained by the concept of the "economic draft." (Legault, "Report to the Minister.")

4 M. Thomas Davis, "Operation Dire Straits: Here's Why the Military Is Failing to Attract the Right Recruits," *Washington Post*, 16 January 2000.

5 Hillen, "Must US Military Culture Reform?" 12.

6 Ulmer et al., *American Military Culture*, xiv, xix, 2, 3, 5.

7 Snider, "Uninformed Debate on Military Culture," 12.

8 Ulmer et al., *American Military Culture*, 7.

9 Holsti, "Widening Gap between the Military and Civilian Society?" Huntington's claim that before the Second World War the US military was generally isolated from American society has recently been challenged. See for example Coffman, "Long Shadow of *The Soldier and the State*."

10 Janowitz, cited in Ricks, "On American Soil."

11 See John M. Olin Institute for Strategic Studies Project on U.S. Post Cold-War Civil-Military Relations, Harvard Univ. for more information. http//www.wcfia.harvard.edu/olin/publications/workingpapers/index.htm

12 William S. Lind et al. in Ricks, "On American Soil."

13 Ricks, "On American Soil."

14 Murray, "Military Culture Does Matter," 36.

15 Fonte, "Anti-Americanization," 48.

16 Weigley, "American Strategy from its Beginnings through the First World War," 412.

17 The *Oxford Concise Dictionary* (6th ed.) defines *pluralism* as a "form of society in which members of minority groups maintain independent traditions."

18 Zoll, "Crisis in Self-Image," 27, 31.

19 Howard, "Men Against Fire," 513–14, 519. Howard cites German colonel Wilhelm Balck, 519.

20 Huntington in panel discussion, John M. Olin Institute for Strategic Studies "A Growing Civil-Military Gap?"

21 Hillen, "Must US Military Culture Reform?" 19.

22 Langston, "Civilian Side of Military Culture," 24.

23 Janowitz surveyed 576 Pentagon staff officers. He found that 21.6 per cent identified themselves as conservative, 45.3 per cent as a little on the conservative side, and 23.1 per cent as a little on the liberal side. Cited in Ricks, "On American Soil."

24 Ricks, "On American Soil."

25 Richard H. Kohn, "General Elections," *Washington Post*, 19 September 2000.

26 Langston, "Civilian Side of Military Culture," 24–5. This is not a new phenomenon in the US military. "'Before World War II, the majority of military posts were located in the South and in the West.' This was also an era when the South was disproportionately represented in the ranks of senior officers–some 90% of Army generals had a 'southern affiliation' in 1910." Ricks and Janowitz cited in Ricks, "On American Soil."

27 Huntington in panel discussion, John M. Olin Institute for Strategic Studies, "A Growing Civil-Military Gap?"

28 Maslowski, "Army Values and American Values," 11.

29 Ibid., 16.

30 Ibid., 11.

31 Langston, "Civilian Side of Military Culture," 22.

32 Maslowski, "Army Values and American Values," 12–14.

33 Ibid., 12.

34 Korb, "The Military and Social Change."

35 Maslowski, "Army Values and American Values," 21.

36 Bland, "Canada's Officer Corps."

37 Huntington in Ricks, "On American Soil."

38 Maslowski, "Army Values and American Values," 22.

39 Langston, "Civilian Side of Military Culture," 22.

40 Breslin, "Organizational Culture and the Military," 3.

41 Bacevitch and Kohn cited in Ricks, "On American Soil."

42 Ricks, "On American Soil."

43 Ibid.

44 Ulmer et al., *American Military Culture*, xx. Quotation from Breslin, "Organizational Culture and the Military," 28.

45 Breslin, "Organizational Culture and the Military," 1, 16.

46 Gabriel and Savage, *Crisis in Command*, 86–8.

47 Marlin, "Cynicism and Careerism," 8.

48 Ulmer et al., *American Military Culture*, xxi–ii, xv, 36–7.

49 The survey was reported by the Secretary of the Army's Senior Review Panel on Sexual Harassment to the US Army War College class of 1998 (Bell, "Impact of Policies on Organizational Values and Culture," 10).

50 Breslin, "Organizational Culture and the Military," 17. Some Canadian soldiers deployed to Croatia showed similar levels of lack of

confidence in their leaders. See Passey and Crockett, "Psychological Consequences of Canadian UN Peacekeeping," 8–9.
51 Breslin, "Organizational Culture and the Military," 18–19, 22, 23.
52 Bell, "Impact of Policies on Organizational Values and Culture," 8.
53 Ibid., 8–10.
54 Ibid., 7, 10.
55 Ulmer et al., *American Military Culture*, 70–2.
56 Snider, "Uninformed Debate on Military Culture," 22.
57 Ulmer et al., *American Military Culture*, xx–ii.
58 Bell, "Impact of Policies on Organizational Values and Culture," 8.
59 A similar situation has been observed in the US Navy. (Dale Eisman, 'Administrivia' Drives Officers out of Navy, Survey Shows," [Hampton, VA] *Virginian-Pilot*, 17 January 2000.)
60 Nelson and Quick, *Organizational Behavior*, 540–1.
61 Ulmer et al., *American Military Culture*, 11.
62 Cited in Breslin, "Organizational Culture and the Military," 29.
63 Maslowski, "Army Values and American Values," 15–16.

CHAPTER FIVE

1 Bercuson, *Significant Incident*, 43.
2 Miller, *Painting the Map Red*, xi, xiv, 366, 437–40; and Miller, "Canadians and the South African War" (presentation given at the Canadian War Museum, Ottawa, 18 November 1999).
3 Bercuson, *Significant Incident*, 43–5.
4 Michael L. Hadley, "Popular Image of the Canadian Navy," 51.
5 Bland, "Canada's Officer Corps."
6 In 1943, 73 per cent of Canadians supported a post-war peacekeeping force even if it meant Canadian servicemen might be killed serving in it. (Morrison and Plain, "The Canadian UN Policy: An Historical Assessment," 167.) Twenty years later 75 per cent of Canadians supported Canadian participation in UN peacekeeping forces. (Paul and Lauglicht, *In Your Opinion*, 16.) I am grateful to Jonathan Eacott of my History 876 graduate seminar for drawing these figures to my attention.
7 Bercuson, *Significant Incident*, 58–60.
8 Kiras, "Maritime Command, National Missions, and Naval Identity," 345.
9 March, "The RCAF and Peacekeeping."
10 Bercuson, *Significant Incident*, 61–2, 64–5.
11 Ibid., 41, 65, 67–8.

12 Crickard, "Strategy, the Fleet-in-Being, and the Strategic Culture of the Officer Corps," 60.
13 Milner, *Canada's Navy*, 72.
14 Michael L. Hadley, "Popular Image of the Canadian Navy," 36–40.
15 Milner, *Canada's Navy*, 177.
16 Michael L. Hadley, "Popular Image of the Canadian Navy," 50.
17 Crickard, "Strategy, the Fleet-in-Being, and the Strategic Culture of the Officer Corps," 57–60.
18 Milner, *Canada's Navy*, 168–71, 173, 175–6, 179, 184, 195.
19 Ibid., 185–6, 269, 285–6, 308.
20 Michael L. Hadley, "Popular Image of the Canadian Navy," 55.
21 Kiras, "Maritime Command, National Missions, and Naval Identity," 341, 348.
22 McCaffery, *Air Aces*, 1.
23 Winter, *First of the Few*, 22.
24 Wise, *Canadian Airmen and the First World War*, 597.
25 Winter, *First of the Few*, 21.
26 Wise, *Canadian Airmen and the First World War*, 113, 117–18.
27 Allan D. English, *Cream of the Crop*, 25.
28 Bingham, *Explorer in the Air Service*, 11–22.
29 Douglas, *Creation of a National Air Force*, 65.
30 Ibid., 138; and Stacey, *Arms, Men and Governments*, 48.
31 Terraine, *Right of the Line*, 258; and Douglas, *Creation of a National Air Force*, 247.
32 Morton, *Military History of Canada*, 225.
33 Allan D. English, *Cream of the Crop*, 141.
34 Foster, *For Love and Glory*, 124; and [Brett Cairns], "Canadian Military Aerospace Power," vol. 1, 21.
35 Granatstein, "American Influence on the Canadian Military," 134.
36 Milner, *Canada's Navy*, 187.
37 Bercuson, *Significant Incident*, 69.
38 Milner, *Canada's Navy*, 236–7.
39 Bercuson, *Significant Incident*, 69–74.
40 Ibid., 75–6.
41 Cotton, "Canadian Military Ethos,"10.
42 See for example, DND, "Review Group on the Report of the Task Force on Unification of the Canadian Forces" (Vance Report); and Directorate of Personnel Development Studies, "Officer Corps Study – Phase One Report – Development of a Framework of Principles."
43 DND, "Ethos and Values in the Canadian Forces."

44 In 1973, Byers and Gray referred to the "poverty of Canadian military thought" and observed that the search for "a more distinctive [Canadian] military ethos" paralleled the "search for identity in other areas of Canadian life." (Byers and Gray, *Canadian Military Professionalism*, 5.)
45 Christopher Moore, "Colonization and Conflict," 183–4.
46 Adrian Preston, "Profession of Arms in Postwar Canada," 194–5, 203, 211; and Morton, *Military History of Canada*, 85, 104, 110.
47 Cotton, "Canadian Military Ethos," 10–13.
48 Flemming, "Hearts and Minds of Soldiers in Canada," 22.
49 Cotton, "Canadian Military Ethos," 12.
50 Directorate of Personnel Development Studies, "Officer Corps Study," pp. 4–1 to 4–4, annex D.
51 Ibid., annex J, p. J-4.
52 Near, "Divining the Message," 66, 79, 86n37, 90–1n81.
53 Bland, "Government of Canada and the Armed Forces," 43.
54 Desmond Morton cited in Hunt and Haycock, *Canada's Defence*, 3.
55 See for example Hunt and Haycock, *Canada's Defence*, 2–3.
56 Adrian Preston, "Profession of Arms in Postwar Canada," 193.
57 Ibid., 204.
58 Ibid., 211; Morton, "Morton Report: What to Tell the Minister" and Douglas, "Why Does Canada Have Armed Forces?" 279, 281–3.
59 Douglas, "Why Does Canada Have Armed Forces?" 282; and Baril, "Speaking Notes for Chief of the Defence Staff."
60 DND, "Shaping the Future of the Canadian Forces," 1–2.
61 Cotton, "Canadian Military Ethos,"13, 15.
62 See for example Loomis and Lightburn, "Taking into Account the Distinctness of the Military from the Mainstream of Society"; and Alain Pellerin, "Demilitarization of the Canadian Forces," letter to the editor, *National Post*, 22 November 1999.
63 Legault, "Report to the Minister."
64 Winslow cited in Castonguay, "Distinguish to Unite," 115.
65 Winslow, "Misplaced Loyalties," 355, 364.
66 Ibid., 345–6, 350.
67 Ibid., 348.
68 Ibid., 353, 357.
69 Ibid., 356–9, 361.
70 Ibid., 364–4.
71 Before unification Canada had three separate services: the RCN, the RCAF, and the Canadian Army. After 1 February 1968, when the Canadian Forces Reorganization Act took effect, all Canada's armed

forces were unified into a single service – the CF. While the RCN, the RCAF, and the Canadian Army no longer existed as legal entities, people often referred to the navy, air force, and army in everyday usage. However, to emphasize the point that Canada no longer had three services, DND bureaucrats coined the rather awkward term "environment," based on the environments in which the sea, air, and land components of the CF operate, to describe these three components of the CF. Since there is only one military service in Canada today – the CF – official DND publications sometimes use the noun "environment" and the adjective "environmental" when referring to the sea, air, and land components of the CF. Nonetheless, the terms Canadian Army, Navy, and Air Force are creeping back, even into official usage. See Critchley, "Civilianization and the Canadian Military," 232–7 for a more detailed explanation of how unification affected the CF.

72 Bland, "Canada's Officer Corps."
73 Near, "Divining the Message," 65.
74 Ibid., 76.
75 Ibid., 67–8, 72–3, 76–7, 83n22, 89n67, 90n74.
76 Wild, "Army Culture," 1, 3, 5, 6–8.
77 Bercuson, *Significant Incident*, 26–7.
78 Wild, "Army Culture," 4.
79 Ibid., 10.
80 Bercuson, *Significant Incident*, 103–5, 112, 114.
81 Allan D. English, "Leadership and Operational Stress in the Canadian Forces," 36–7.
82 Wild, "Army Culture," 8–10, 18.
83 Nelson and Quick, *Organizational Behavior*, 540–1.

CHAPTER SIX

1 Castonguay, "Distinguish to Unite," 96–7, 106–11, 116.
2 Berton, *Why We Act Like Canadians*, 16, 42, 45.
3 Michael Adams, *Sex in the Snow*, xv–xvii, xix–xxii, 6–7, 18, 19, 32, 40.
4 Mergen, "?American? Studies," 6.
5 Hull, "From Many, Two," 4, 22.
6 Courchene, "Canada and the Emerging Global Order" (presentation to National Securities Study Seminar 9901, CFC, Toronto, 6 May 1999).
7 Abramson et al., "Cross-national Cognitive Process Differences," 123; and Soeters and Recht, "Culture and Discipline in Military Academies," 178.

8 Dale Eisman, "'Administrivia' Drives Officers out of Navy, Survey Shows," (Hampton, VA) *Virginian-Pilot*, 17 January 2000; and Flammer, "Conflicting Loyalties and the American Military Ethic," 164–5. Flammer discusses the deleterious effects that "zero defects" philosophies have had in the past on the US military.

9 Jockel, "Canada and International Peacekeeping," 155.

10 Barry and Thomas, "Not Your Father's Army," 48.

11 Michael Adams, *Sex in the Snow*, 21.

12 Hillen, "Must US Military Culture Reform?" 11; Murray, "Military Culture Does Matter," 32; Winslow, "Misplaced Loyalties," 345; and James M. Smith, "Air Force Culture and Cohesion," 41.

13 Winslow, "Misplaced Loyalties," 345; Macmillan, "Strategic Culture and National Ways in Warfare," 33; and Hillen, "Must US Military Culture Reform?" 11. Quote from Winslow, "Misplaced Loyalties."

14 Ulmer et al., *American Military Culture*, 65.

15 Builder, *Masks of War*, 3, 39.

16 Builder, *Icarus Syndrome*, 5–6.

17 Ulmer et al., *American Military Culture*, 13.

18 Ibid., 10–13.

19 James M. Smith, "Air Force Culture and Cohesion," 50, 51.

20 Ibid., 45, 51–2.

21 Ibid., 43, 45, 47–52.

22 US Department of Defense, Joint Publication 0–2, *Unified Action Armed Forces*, 11, 13, 15.

23 Snider, "Uninformed Debate on Military Culture," 15, 20.

24 Swain, "Filling the Void," 148–66, gives an excellent summary of the process that led to the development of the operational art concept in the US Army. The US Army defines *operational art* as the "employment of military forces to attain strategic goals in a theatre of war or theatre of operations." Ibid., 165.

25 Sloan, *Revolution in Military Affairs*, 33–4, 35–7, 45–7 (quotations); and Morneau, "US Joint Doctrine." See Van Riper and Scales, "Preparing for War in the 21st Century," 4–14, for a summary of the US Army and Marine Corps focus on surface warfare and the concept of air power as a battlefield support function.

26 A.C. Zinni, "Verbatim," *Washington Post Online*, 16 July 2000.

27 Sapolsky, "Interservice Competition," 51.

28 Builder, *Masks of War*, 3.

29 Sapolsky, "Interservice Competition," 51–3.

30 For an overview of this question and current problems, see Bland, "Government of Canada and the Armed Forces," 27–45.
31 Dewar, "Impact of the Evolution of the Operational Level of War."
32 Adrian Preston, "Profession of Arms in Postwar Canada," 203.
33 Granatstein, "American Influence on the Canadian Military," 134–5; and Boomer, "Joint or Combined Doctrine?"
34 Dewar, "Impact of the Evolution of the Operational Level of War."
35 Semianiw, "Western Operational Theory."
36 See for example Eddy, "Canadian Forces and the Operational Level of War," 18–24.
37 Dewar, "Impact of the Evolution of the Operational Level of War."
38 Boomer, "Joint or Combined Doctrine?"
39 Dewar, "Impact of the Evolution of the Operational Level of War."
40 Ibid.
41 MacGillivary et al., "Inter-Service Cooperation," 192–3.
42 Calvin, "Joint HQ Planning Process," and Jurkowski, "Canadian Joint Doctrine" (presentations to AMSC 2, 20 September 1999); and Boomer, "Joint or Combined Doctrine?"
43 Morton, "Morton Report: What to Tell the Minister."
44 A.C. Okros, "The Gaps Between Military and Civilian Societies," 7.
45 Ibid., 8, 11.
46 DND, "Shaping the Future of the Canadian Forces," 1–2.
47 Cotton, "Canadian Military Ethos,"13, 15.
48 Bercuson, *Significant Incident*, 26.
49 Cotton, "Canadian Military Ethos,"13.
50 Steven Lee Myers, "Reservists' New Role Transforms Military," *New York Times on the Web*, 24 January, 2000.
51 Moskos, "Toward a Postmodern Military," 23.
52 Ulmer et al., *American Military Culture*, xix.
53 Ibid., 8, xxi–ii.
54 Hillen, "Must US Military Culture Reform?" 14; and Richard Preston, "Potential of the Military for Contributions," 70.
55 Moskos, "Toward a Postmodern Military," 18.
56 Pinch, "Canada: Managing Change with Shrinking Resources," 159.
57 Morton, *Military History of Canada*, 238; and Pinch, "Canada: Managing Change with Shrinking Resources," 159.
58 Moskos, "Toward a Postmodern Military," 22–4.
59 Pinch, "Canada: Managing Change with Shrinking Resources," 165–9.

60 Summerskill, "It's Official: Gays Do Not Harm Forces," *Observer*, 19 November 2000.
61 Morton, *Military History of Canada*, 228; and Morton, "Brief on the History of the CFC."
62 Galbraith, "A Liberal's Debt to Canadians," 40.

CHAPTER SEVEN

1 Szafranski, "Peer Competitors, the RMA," 116.
2 Biddle, "Victory Misunderstood," 141.
3 Cited in Caldwell, "Promises, Promises," 56.
4 Reimer, "Dominant Maneuver and Precision Engagement," 16.
5 Lind et al., "Changing Face of War," 2–11.
6 Metz, "Wake for Clausewitz."
7 Van Creveld, "High Technology and the Transformation of War, Part 2," 61–4.
8 Murray, "Thinking About Revolutions in Military Affairs," 69; and John A. English, *Marching Through Chaos*, 10.
9 Baumann, "Historical Perspectives on Future War," 44–5.
10 Cohen, "Revolution in Warfare," 52–3.
11 Baumann, "Historical Perspectives on Future War," 44–5.
12 John A. English, *Marching Through Chaos*, 50.
13 O'Connell, *Of Arms and Men*, 11.
14 John A. English, *Marching Through Chaos*, 19, 33, 50.
15 Ibid., 61–4.
16 Mandeles et al., *Managing "Command and Control" in the Persian Gulf War*, 1, 149–56.
17 Murray, "Thinking About Revolutions in Military Affairs," 70, 73.
18 Biddle, 140, 178, 179.
19 Sloan, "The United States and the Revolution in Military Affairs," 15.
20 US Department of Defense, Joint Publication 0–2, *Unified Action Armed Forces*, 11, 13, 15.
21 Szafranski, "Annulling Marriages," 118.
22 Cohen, "Revolution in Warfare," 48.
23 Cited in Lefebvre et al, "'Revolution in Military Affairs,'" 179.
24 Builder, "Looking in All the Wrong Places?" 39.
25 Cohen, "Revolution in Warfare," 37.
26 Kasurak, "Civilianization and the Military Ethos," 116.
27 Mileham, "Future of Military Leadership," 51.
28 Ibid., 48–50.

29 Ibid., 51.
30 Ibid., 52.
31 Ibid., 51–4.
32 Ibid., 54.
33 Ibid., 55–8.
34 Oliver, "Canadian Military Professional Development."
35 Bland, "Canada's Officer Corps."
36 Oliver, "Canadian Military Professional Development."
37 Weigley, *American Way of War*, 359; Andre, "National Culture and Warfare," 104–5; and Martin P. Adams, "Peace Enforcement versus American Strategic Culture," 16.
38 Martin P. Adams, "Peace Enforcement versus American Strategic Culture," 21; and Johnston, "Myth of Manoeuvre Warfare," 29.
39 Andre, "National Culture and Warfare," 107.
40 Mackubin Thomas Owens, "Military Ethos and 'Don't Ask, Don't Tell."
41 Bland, "Canada's Officer Corps."
42 Ulmer et al., *American Military Culture*, xxii–iii.
43 Rowan Scarborough, "Army Survey Rebuts Pentagon," *Washington Times*, 10 January 2000.
44 Near, "Divining the Message," 69, 74, 84n24.
45 Freakley et al., "Training for Peace Support Operations," 17.
46 See for example Freakley et al., "Training for Peace Support Operations," 17–24; and Cran, "Training For Peace Operations," 18.
47 See Walsh, "Operations Other than War and Its Impact on Combat Training Readiness," 2, 13, 24, 26; and Blankmeyer, "Sustaining Combat Readiness During Peace Operations," 3, 7, 10, 29.
48 Cuningham, "Ellerbe's Career on line after Unit's Actions in Kosovo," *Fayetteville (NC) Observer*, 8 October 2000.
49 Moskos in John M. Olin Institute for Strategic Studies, "Growing Civil-Military Gap?"
50 Hillen, "Must US Military Culture Reform?" 14.
51 Buschmann, "Sustaining Peacekeeping Forces," 3–14. See also LaRose-Edwards et al., *Non-Military Training for Canadian Peacekeepers*.
52 See Melakopides, *Pragmatic Idealism*, for a full discussion of this concept.
53 Castonguay, "Distinguish to Unite," 101.
54 Watson, *Globalization and the Meaning of Canadian Life*, x, 215 (quotation).
55 Ibid., 237–41, 255.
56 Michael Adams, *Sex in the Snow*, 171–3, 175, 178.

57 Buschert, "DND Looks into the Future"; and Hills, "Military in a Changing Society."
58 Castonguay, "Distinguish to Unite," 112.
59 Hills, "Military in a Changing Society."
60 Ibid.
61 Bercuson, *Significant Incident*, 99–100.
62 Castonguay, "Distinguish to Unite," 113–14.
63 Major-General Thomas De Faye cited in Bercuson, *Significant Incident*, 88.
64 Michael Adams, *Sex in the Snow*, 102.
65 Wild, "Army Culture," 3, 5.
66 Moskos et al., "Armed Forces after the Cold War," 6, 9.
67 Peters, "Why is Strategy Difficult – In Canada?"
68 A. Okros, "Into the 21st Century: Strategic HR Issues." The substance of this report is published in Bland, *Backbone of the Army*, 25–46.
69 Wood, "Vanishing Border," 22.
70 Wallace, "What Makes a Canadian?" 33. See Granatstein, *Yankee Go Home*, for a historical survey of these issues.
71 Howard, "Military Science in the Age of Peace," 3–4.
72 Ulmer et al., *American Military Culture*, 47, 49, 58–9. Quotation from p. 58.
73 Ibid., 61.
74 Bell, "Impact of Policies on Organizational Values and Culture," 6–7, 9, 11–12; and Ulmer et al., *American Military Culture*, xxvi.
75 For example, a recent report of the Minister's Monitoring Committee on Change in the Department of National Defence indicated that, while certain educational initiatives are proceeding in the CF, "a central plan was absent." (Minister's Monitoring Committee on Change in the Department of National Defence and the Canadian Forces "Second Interim Report of the Minister's Monitoring Committee on Change," chapter 5.)

CHAPTER EIGHT

1 Ulmer et al., *American Military Culture*, xv.
2 Johnston, "Doctrine Is Not Enough," 30.
3 Byers and Gray, "Preface," 5.
4 Moskos et al., "Armed Forces after the Cold War," 6, 9.
5 Soeters and Recht, "Culture and Discipline in Military Academies," 179, 183.

Bibliography

Abramson, Neil R., et al. "Cross-national Cognitive Process Differences: A Comparison of Canadian, American and Japanese Managers." *Management International Review* 36, no. 2 (1996): 123–39.

Adams, Martin P. "Peace Enforcement versus American Strategic Culture." *Strategic Review* 23, no. 1 (Winter 1995): 14–22.

Adams, Michael. *Sex in the Snow: Canadian Social Values at the End of the Millennium*. Toronto: Penguin Books, 1998.

Andre, David J. "National Culture and Warfare–Whither Decisive Force." *Joint Force Quarterly* no. 13 (Autumn 1996): 104–8.

Bachman, Jerald G., et al. "Distinctive Attitudes among US Enlistees, 1976–1997: Self-Selection versus Socialization." *Armed Forces & Society* 26, no. 4 (Summer 2000): 561–85.

Baril, Maurice. "Keynote Address: The State of the Profession of Arms in the Canadian Forces." Paper presented at Conference of Defence Associations Institute XVth Annual Seminar, 1999 – The Profession of Arms in Canada: Past, Present and Future. http://www.cda-cdai.ca/english-frame.htm

– "Speaking Notes for Chief of the Defence Staff – Secondary Schools United Nations Symposium." Montreal, 12 November 1999. A copy of the speech can be obtained from Public Affairs Headquarters, National Defence Headquarters, MGen George R. Pearkes Bldg, 15 NT, 101 Colonel By Drive, Ottawa, ON K1A 0K2.

Barry, John and Evan Thomas. "Not Your Father's Army: Does America need Faster Striking Power or Bigger Guns?" *Newsweek*, 22 November 1999.

Barzun, Jacques, "The Professions Under Siege." In Malham M. Wakin, ed. *War, Morality, and the Military Profession*, 2nd ed., 121–33. London: Westview Press, 1986.

Baumann, Robert F. "Historical Perspectives on Future War." *Military Review* 76, no. 2 (March–April 1997): 40–8.

Beauchamp, Major Denis. "The Fundamentals of Canadian Defence Ethics." August 1997. http://www.dnd.ca/ethics/pages/kdocs_e.htm#articles

Bell, William F. "The Impact of Policies on Organizational Values and Culture." Paper presented at the Joint Services Conference on Professional Ethics (January 1999). http://www.usafa.af.mil/jscope/JSCOPE99/Bell99.html

Ben-Eliezer, Uri. *The Making of Israeli Militarism*. Bloomington: Indiana Univ. Press, 1998.

Bercuson, David. *Significant Incident: Canada's Army, the Airborne, and the Murder in Somalia.* Toronto: McClelland & Stewart, 1996.

Berton, Pierre. *Why We Act Like Canadians*. Toronto: McClelland & Stewart, 1982.

Biddle, Stephen. "Victory Misunderstood: What the Gulf War Tells Us about the Future of Conflict." *International Security* 21, no. 2 (Fall 1996): 139–79.

Bingham, Hiram. *An Explorer in the Air Service.* New Haven: Yale Univ. Press, 1920.

Bland, Douglas L. *Backbone of the Army: Non-Commissioned Officers in the Future Army.* Montreal & Kingston: McGill-Queen's Univ. Press, 2000.

– "Canada's Officer Corps: New Times, New Ideas." Paper presented at Conference of Defence Associations Institute XVth Annual Seminar, 1999 – The Profession of Arms in Canada: Past, Present and Future. http://www.cda-cdai.ca/english-frame.htm

– "The Government of Canada and the Armed Forces: A Troubled Relationship." In David A. Charters and J. Brent Wilson, eds. *The Soldier and the Canadian State: A Crisis in Civil-Military Relations?* 27–45. Fredericton, NB: Centre for Conflict Studies, 1996.

Blankmeyer, William J. "Sustaining Combat Readiness During Peace Operations." Carlisle Barracks, PA: US Army War College, 1998.

Boomer, F.M. "Joint or Combined Doctrine?: The Right Choice for Canada." Paper prepared for Advanced Military Studies Course (AMSC) 1, 1998. Available from Information Resource Centre, Canadian Forces College, Toronto. http://bib.cfc.dnd.ca/webpacj/cfc.html

Breslin, Charles B. "Organizational Culture and the Military." Carlisle Barracks, PA: US Army War College, 2000.

Broadbent, David. "Military Society, Change or Decay, Part 1 & 2." *Canadian Defence Quarterly* 11, no. 4, (Spring 1982): 24–7; and 12, no. 1 (Summer 1982): 28–30.

Brown, Craig, ed. *The Illustrated History of Canada*. Toronto: Lester, 1996.

Builder, Carl H. *The Icarus Syndrome: The Role of Air Power Theory in the Evolution and Fate of the US Air Force*. London: Transaction Publishers, 1994.

– "Looking in All the Wrong Places?" *Armed Forces Journal International* (May 1995): 38–9.

– *The Masks of War: American Military Styles in Strategy and Analysis*. Baltimore: Johns Hopkins Univ. Press, 1989.

Burk, James. "Expertise, Jurisdiction, and Legitimacy of the Military Profession." Paper presented at the Inter-University Seminar on Armed Forces and Society, Baltimore, MD, 19–21 October 2001.

Buschert, Heather. "DND Looks into the Future." VCDS Defence 2000, [January 1998]. http://www.vcds.dnd.ca/dgsp/dsc/D2000nws/1998/jan98/future_e.asp

Buschmann, Klaus. "Training and Education: Essential Prerequisites for Sustainability in Operations Other than War." Paper prepared for AMSC 3, 2000. Available from Information Resource Centre, Canadian Forces College, Toronto. (Not available electronically.)

Byers, R.B. and Colin S. Gray. Preface in *Canadian Military Professionalism: The Search for Identity.* Toronto: Canadian Institute of International Affairs, 1973.

[Cairns, Brett]. *Canadian Military Aerospace Power.* Vol. 1. Toronto: Canadian Forces College, nd.

Caldwell, Warren Jr. "Promises, Promises." *US Naval Institute Proceedings* 122 (January 1996): 54–7.

Calvin, James. "Joint HQ Planning Process." Presentation to AMSC 2, 20 September 1999.

Capstick, M.D. "Defining the Culture: The Canadian Army in the 21st Century." Paper presented at the Inter-University Seminar on Armed Forces and Society, Baltimore, MD, 19–21 October 2001.

Castonguay, Jacques. "Distinguish to Unite or Leadership in the Canadian Forces at the Start of the Third Millennium." In Bernd Horn, ed. *Contemporary Issues in Officership: A Canadian Perspective*, 93–122. Toronto: Canadian Institute for Strategic Studies, 2000.

Cock, Jacklyn and Laurie Nathan. *War and Society: The Militarisation of South Africa.* Cape Town and Johannesburg: David Philip, 1989.

Coffman, Edward M. "The Long Shadow of *The Soldier and the State.*" *The Journal of Military History* 55 (January 1991): 69–82.

Cohen, Eliot A. "A Revolution in Warfare." *Foreign Affairs* 75, no. 2 (March/April 1996): 37–54.

Commission of Inquiry into the Deployment of Canadian Forces to Somalia. *Dishonoured Legacy: The Lessons of the Somalia Affair.* Report of the

Commission. Ottawa: Minister of Public Works and Government Services, 1997.

Corum, James S. "A Clash of Military Cultures: German and French Approaches to Technology between the World Wars." United States. Joint Chiefs of Staff Joint Doctrine Web site. http://www.dtic.mil/doctrine/research_publications.htm

Cotton, C.A. "A Canadian Military Ethos." *Canadian Defence Quarterly* 12, no. 3 (Winter 1982/83): 10–18.

– "Military Attitudes and Values of the Army in Canada." CFPARU Report 79-5. Willowdale, ON: CF Personnel Applied Research Unit, 1979.

Courchene, Thomas. "Canada and the Emerging Global Order." Presentation to National Securities Study Seminar 9901, CFC, Toronto, 6 May 1999.

Cran, Christopher J. "Training For Peace Operations: The U.S. Army Adapts to the Post-Cold War." Review of J. Michael Hardesty and Jason D. Ellis, *Training for Peace Operations: The U.S. Army Adapts to the Post-Cold War World*. In *Peacekeeping and International Relations* 27, no. 1 (January/February 1998): 18.

Crickard, Fred W. "Strategy, the Fleet-in-Being, and the Strategic Culture of the Officer Corps." In Michael L. Hadley, et al., eds. *A Nation's Navy: In Quest of Canadian Naval Identity*, 57–70. Montreal & Kingston: McGill-Queen's Univ. Press, 1996.

Critchley, Harriet W. "Civilianization and the Canadian Military." In B.D. Hunt and R.G. Haycock, eds. *Canada's Defence*, 198–210. Toronto: Copp Clark Pitman, 1993.

Czerwinski, Thomas J. "Command and Control at the Crossroads." *Parameters* 26, no. 3 (Autumn 1996): 121–32.

Dewar, J.S. "The Impact of the Evolution of the Operational Level of War on the Structure of the Canadian Forces: a Sailor's Perspective." Paper prepared for AMSC 1, 1998. Available from Information Resource Centre, Canadian Forces College, Toronto. http//198.231.69.12/papers/amsc1/index.html

Directorate of Personnel Development Studies. "Officer Corps Study – Phase One Report – Development of a Framework of Principles." Ottawa: DND, 1989.

DND. "Canada's Army," B-GL-300-000/FP-000, Ottawa: DND, 1998.

– *Canadian Forces Operations*, B-GG-005-004/AF-000. http://www.forces.gc.ca/dcds/jointDoc/pages/keydocs_e.asp. Then select *Canadian Forces Operations* from the list.

– Ethos and Values in the Canadian Forces." 1997. http//www.forces.gc.ca/site/minister/eng/Ethos/ETHMAR19.htm

– "Review Group on the Report of the Task Force on Unification of the Canadian Forces" (Vance Report). Ottawa: DND, 1980.

– "Second Interim Report of the Minister's Monitoring Committee on Change in the Department of National Defence and the Canadian Forces," [July 1999]. (Article retitled on Web site as "Minister's Monitoring Committee on Change in the Department of National Defence and the Canadian Forces: Interim Report – 1999.") http://www.forces.gc.ca/site/reports/monitor_com/eng/cover_e.htm

– "Shaping the Future of the Canadian Forces: A Strategy for 2020." (June 1999). http://www.cds.forces.gc.ca/pubs/strategy2k/intro_e.asp

DND. Special Review Group. "Detailed Report of the Special Review Group-Operation Harmony (Rotation Two)." 16 June 2000. http://www.forces.gc.ca/site/reports/harmony_2/index-e.htm

Douglas, W.A.B. *Creation of a National Air Force.* Vol. 2 of *The Official History of the Royal Canadian Air Force.* Toronto: Univ. of Toronto Press, 1986.

– "Why Does Canada Have Armed Forces?" *International Journal* 30, no. 2 (Spring 1975): 259–83.

Eddy, K.T. "The Canadian Forces and the Operational Level of War." *Canadian Defence Quarterly* 5 (April 1992): 18–24.

Edmonds, Martin. *Armed Services and Society.* Boulder, CO: Westview Press, 1990.

English, Allan D., ed. *The Changing Face of War: Learning from History.* Montreal & Kingston: McGill-Queen's Univ. Press, 1998.

– *The Cream of the Crop: Canadian Aircrew 1939–1945.* Montreal & Kingston: McGill-Queen's Univ. Press, 1996.

– "Leadership and Operational Stress in the Canadian Forces." *Canadian Military Journal* 1, no. 3 (Autumn 2000): 33–8.

English, John A. *Marching Through Chaos: The Descent of Armies in Theory and Practice.* Westport, CT: Praeger, 1996.

Feaver, Peter D. "The Civil-Military Problematique: Huntington, Janowitz, and the Question of Civilian Control." *Armed Forces and Society* 23, no. 2 (Winter 1996): 149–78.

Ferrill, Arthur. "Elite Forces in the Ancient World." In A. Hamish Ion and Keith Neilson, eds, *Elite Military Formations in War and Peace,* 31–42. Westport, CT: Praeger, 1996.

Finer, Samuel. *The Man on Horseback: The Role of the Military in Politics.* New York: Praeger, 1962.

Flammer, Philip M. "Conflicting Loyalties and the American Military Ethic." In Malham M. Waking, ed. *War, Morality, and the Military Profession*, 2nd ed., 157–70. London: Westview Press, 1986.

Flemming, S.B. "The Hearts and Minds of Soldiers in Canada: The Military Ethos Scale (MES) in Retrospect." DSEA Staff Note 89/01. Ottawa: Operational Research and Analysis Establishment, Directorate of Social and Economic Analysis, 1989.

Fonte, John. "Anti-Americanization." *National Review* 48 (2 September 1996), 48–53.

Foster, J.A. *For Love and Glory*. Toronto: McClelland & Stewart, 1989.

Freakley, Benjamin C., et al. "Training for Peace Support Operations." *Military Review* 78, no. 4 (July–August 1998): 17–24.

Gabriel, Richard and Paul Savage. *Crisis in Command: Mismanagement in the Army*. New York: Hill and Wang, 1978.

Galbraith, John Kenneth, "A Liberal's Debt to Canadians," *Maclean's*, 2 August 1999, 40.

Gilbert, Felix. "Machiavelli." In Peter Paret, ed. *Makers of Modern Strategy*, 11–31. Princeton: Princeton Univ. Press, 1986.

Goetze, Bernd A. "Military Professionalism: The Canadian Officer Corps." Paper prepared for the Centre for International Relations, Queen's University Kingston, National Security Series no. 3, 1976.

Granatstein, J.L. "The American Influence on the Canadian Military." In B.D. Hunt and R.G. Haycock, eds. *Canada's Defence*, 129–39. Toronto: Copp Clark Pitman, 1993.

– *Yankee Go Home*. Toronto: HarperCollins, 1996.

Grant, Rebecca. "Closing the Doctrine Gap." *Air Force Magazine* 80, no. 1 (January 1997): 48–52.

Hadley, Arthur T. *The Straw Giant*. New York: Random House, 1986.

Hadley, Michael L. The Popular Image of the Canadian Navy." In Michael L. Hadley, et al., eds. *A Nation's Navy: In Quest of Canadian Naval Identity*, 35–56. Montreal & Kingston: McGill-Queen's Univ. Press, 1996.

Hadley, Michael L., et al., eds. *A Nation's Navy: In Quest of Canadian Naval Identity*. Montreal & Kingston: McGill-Queen's Univ. Press, 1996.

Haydon, Peter T. "The Changing Nature of Canadian Civil-Military Relations in the Aftermath of the Cold War." In David A. Charters and J. Brent Wilson, eds. *The Soldier and the Canadian State: A Crisis in Civil-Military Relations?* 46–64. Fredericton, NB: Centre for Conflict Studies, 1996.

Hillen, John. "Must US Military Culture Reform?" *Parameters* 29, no. 3 (Autumn 1999): 9–23.

Hills, R.L. "The Military in a Changing Society: The Impact of Demographics on the Canadian Forces." Unpublished paper written for CF Command and Staff Course, 1998. http://wps.cfc.dnd.ca/irc/nh/nh9798/0043.html

Holsti, Ole R. "A Widening Gap Between the Military and Civilian Society? Some Evidence, 1976–1996." John M. Olin Institute for Strategic Studies Project on U.S. Post Cold-War Civil-Military Relations, Harvard Univ., October 1997. http://www.wcfia.harvard.edu/olin/publications/workingpapers/index.htm

Horn, Bernd, ed. *Contemporary Issues in Officership: A Canadian Perspective.* Toronto: Canadian Institute for Strategic Studies, 2000.

Howard, Michael. "Men Against Fire: The Doctrine of the Offensive in 1914." In Peter Paret, ed. *Makers of Modern Strategy,* 510–26. Princeton: Princeton Univ. Press, 1986.

– "Military Science in the Age of Peace." *RUSI Journal* 119, no. 1 (March 1974): 3–11.

Hull, James P. "From Many, Two: A Bibliographic History of Canadian-American Relations." *American Studies International* 36, no. 2 (June 1998): 4–22.

Hunt, B.D. and R.G. Haycock, eds. *Canada's Defence.* Toronto: Copp Clark Pitman, 1993.

Huntington, Samuel P. "Officership as a Profession." In Malham M. Wakin, ed. *War, Morality, and the Military Profession*, 2nd ed., 23–34. London: Westview Press, 1986.

– *The Soldier and the State: The Theory and Politics of Civil-Military Relations*. Cambridge, MA: Belknap Press, 1957.

Iverson, Noel. "Rationalization of Warfare and the Military Profession: Effects on Ethics and Civil-Military Relations." In David A. Charters and J. Brent Wilson, eds. *The Soldier and the Canadian State: A Crisis in Civil-Military Relations?* 7–26. Fredericton, NB: Centre for Conflict Studies, 1996.

Janowitz, Morris. *The Professional Soldier.* New York: The Free Press, 1960.

Jockel, Joseph. "Canada and International Peacekeeping: An American View." In Alex Morrison, ed. *The New Peacekeeping Partnership*, 153–8. Cornwallis: Canadian Peacekeeping Press, 1995.

John M. Olin Institute for Strategic Studies. "A Growing Civil-Military Gap? Wrap-Up Panel Discussion of the Olin Institute's U.S. Military and Post–Cold War American Society Project." John M. Olin Institute for Strategic Studies Project on U.S. Post Cold-War Civil-Military Relations, Harvard Univ. (discussion held 26 October 1997, published October 1998). http://www.wcfia.harvard.edu/olin/publications/workingpapers/index.htm

Johns, Gary. *Organizational Behavior*, 2d. Boston: Scott, Foresman, 1988.

Johnston, Paul. "Doctrine Is Not Enough: The Effect of Doctrine on the Behavior of Armies." *Parameters* 30, no. 3 (Autumn 2000): 30–9.

– "The Myth of Manoeuvre Warfare." In Allan D. English, ed. *The Changing Face of War: Learning from History*, 22–32. Montreal & Kingston: McGill-Queen's Univ. Press, 1998.

Jurowski, David. "Canadian Joint Doctrine." Presentation to AMSC 2, 20 September 1999.

Kasurak, Peter C. "Civilianization and the Military Ethos: Civil-Military Relations in Canada." *Canadian Public Administration* 25, no. 1 (Spring 1982): 108–29.

Keegan, John. *A History of Warfare*. Toronto: Vintage Books, 1993.

Kellett, Anthony. "Ceremonial and the Regimental Ethos." DSEA Staff Note 87/01. Ottawa: Operational Research and Analysis Establishment, Directorate of Social and Economic Analysis, 1987.

– "The Role of Territorial Affiliation in the Development of the Regimental Ethos." DSEA Staff Note 85-23. Ottawa: Operational Research and Analysis Establishment, Directorate of Social and Economic Analysis, 1985.

– "The Influence of Unit Appointments in the Development of a Regimental Ethos." DSEA Staff Note 85-07. Ottawa: Operational Research and Analysis Establishment, Directorate of Social and Economic Analysis, 1985.

Kiras, James D. "Maritime Command National Missions, and Naval Identity." In Michael L. Hadley, et al., eds. *A Nation's Navy: In Quest of Canadian Naval Identity*, 339–50. Montreal & Kingston: McGill-Queen's Univ. Press, 1996.

Kohn, Richard H. "General Elections." *Washington Post*, 19 September 2000.

Korb, Lawrence J. "The Military and Social Change." John M. Olin Institute for Strategic Studies Project on U.S. Post Cold-War Civil-Military Relations, Harvard Univ., August 1996. http://www.wcfia.harvard.edu/olin/publications/workingpapers/index.htm

Langston, Thomas S. "The Civilian Side of Military Culture." *Parameters* 30, no. 3 (Autumn 2000): 21–9.

LaRose-Edwards, Paul, et al. *Non-Military Training for Canadian Peacekeepers: A Study Prepared for the Commission of Inquiry into the Deployment of Canadian Forces to Somalia*. Ottawa: Minister of Public Works and Government Services Canada, 1997.

Lefebvre, Stephane, et al. "'The Revolution in Military Affairs': Its Implications for Doctrine and Force Development Within the US Army."

In B.J.C. McKercher and Michael A. Hennessy, eds. *The Operational Art: Developments in the Theories of War*, 173–92. Westport, CT: Praeger, 1996.

Legault, Albert. "Report to the Minister, Part 2: Canadian Society and the Canadian Armed Forces." http://www.forces.gc.ca/site/minister/eng/Legault/Legault_cont_e.htm

Lerner, Max. "The Shame of the Professions." In Malham M. Wakin, ed. *War, Morality, and the Military Profession*, 2d., 134–9. London: Westview Press, 1986.

Lind, William S., et al. "The Changing Face of War: Into the Fourth Generation," *Military Review* 69 (October 1989): 2–21.

Loomis, D.C. and D.T. Lightburn. "Taking into Account the Distinctness of the Military from the Mainstream of Society." *Canadian Defence Quarterly* 10, no. 2 (Autumn 1980): 16–21.

MacGillivary, D., et al. "Inter-Service Cooperation: Is it the Essence of Joint Doctrine?" In David Rudd, et al., eds. *Air Power at the Turn of the Millennium*, 179–95. Toronto: Canadian Institute of Strategic Studies, 1999.

Macmillan, Alan. "Strategic Culture and National Ways in Warfare: The British Case." *Journal of the Royal United Services Institute* 140, no. 5 (October 1995): 33–8.

Mandeles, Mark, et al. *Managing "Command and Control" in the Persian Gulf War*. Westport, CT: Praeger, 1996.

March, Bill. "The RCAF and Peacekeeping." In Office of Air Force Heritage and History, ed., *Proceedings: 6th Annual Air Force Historical Conference*. Winnipeg: Air Force History and Heritage, 2000.

Marlin, John. "Cynicism and Careerism; Threats to Army Ethics." *Army* 47 no. 5 (May 1997): 7–10.

Martin, Joanne. *Cultures in Organizations: Three Perspectives*. New York: Oxford Univ. Press, 1992.

Maslowski, Peter. "Army Values and American Values." *Military Review* 70, no. 4 (April 1990): 10–23.

McCaffery, Dan. *Air Aces: The Lives and Times of Twelve Canadian Fighter Pilots*. Toronto: Lorimer, 1990.

Melakopides, Costas. *Pragmatic Idealism: Canadian Foreign Policy 1945–1995*. Montreal & Kingston: McGill-Queen's Univ. Press, 1998.

Mergen, Bernard. "?American? Studies: A Dialogue Across the Americas." *American Studies International* 37, no. 3 (October 1999): 5–17.

Metz, Steven. "A Wake for Clausewitz: Toward a Philosophy of 21st-Century Warfare." *Parameters* (Winter 1994–95): 126–32.

Mileham, Patrick. "The Future of Military Leadership." In Patrick Mileham and Lee Willett, eds. *Ethical Dilemmas of Military Interventions*, 49–59. London: Royal Institute of International Affairs, 1999.

– "Military Virtues 1: The Right to be Different?" *Defense Analysis* 14, no. 2 (1998): 169–90.

– "Military Virtues 2: The British Army Ethos" *Defense Analysis* 14, no. 3 (1998): 227–46.

Miller, Carmen. "Canadians and the South African War." Presentation given at the Canadian War Museum, Ottawa, 18 November 1999.

– *Painting the Map Red: Canada and the South African War 1899–1902*. Montreal & Kingston: McGill-Queen's Univ. Press, 1993.

Milner, Marc. *Canada's Navy: The First Century*. Toronto: Univ. of Toronto Press, 1999.

Moore, Christopher. "Colonization and Conflict." In Craig Brown, ed. *The Illustrated History of Canada*, 105–88. Toronto: Lester, 1996.

Moore, John. "Renewing DND's Culture: Lessons for the Way Ahead," *Vanguard* 4, no. 3 [1999]: 10–12.

Morneau, J.J. "US Joint Doctrine: Services Influence and 'Disjointness.'" Paper prepared for AMSC 1, 1998. Available from Information Resource Centre, Canadian Forces College, Toronto. http://198.231.69.12/papers/amsc1/index.html

Morrison, Alex and Suzanne M. Plain. "The Canadian UN Policy: An Historical Assessment." In Hans-Georg Ehrart and David G. Haglund, eds. *The "New Peacekeeping" and European Security*, 163–78. Baden-Baden: Nomos Veragsgesellschaft, 1993.

Morton, Desmond. "A Brief on the History of the CFC." http://www.cfc.dnd.ca/history.en.html

– *A Military History of Canada*. Edmonton: Hurtig Publishers, 1985.

– "Morton Report: What to Tell the Minister." http://www.forces.gc.ca/site/minister/eng/Morton/MORTONe.htm

Moskos, Charles C. et al. "Armed Forces after the Cold War." In Charles C. Moskos et al., eds. *The Postmodern Military: Armed Forces After the Cold War*, 1–13. New York: Oxford Univ. Press, 2000.

– eds. *The Postmodern Military: Armed Forces After the Cold War*. New York: Oxford Univ. Press, 2000.

Murray, Williamson. "Military Culture Does Matter." *Strategic Review* 27, no. 2 (Spring 1999): 32–40.

– "Thinking About Revolutions in Military Affairs." *Joint Force Quarterly*, no. 16 (Summer 1997): 69–76.

Near, Robert. "Divining the Message: An Analysis of the MND and Somalia Commission Reports." In Bernd Horn, ed. *Contemporary Issues in Officership: A Canadian Perspective*, 65–92. Toronto: Canadian Institute for Strategic Studies, 2000.

Nelson, Debra L. and James Campbell Quick. *Organizational Behavior: Foundations, Realities, and Challenges*. Cincinnati: South-Western College Publishing, 1999.

O'Connell, Robert L. *Of Arms and Men: A History of War, Weapons, and Aggression*. New York: Oxford Univ. Press, 1989.

Okros, A. "Into the 21st Century: Strategic HR Issues." A Defence Management Committee Discussion Paper. http://www.vcds.dnd.ca/dgsp/analysis/hr_e.asp

Okros, A.C. "The Gaps Between Military and Civilian Societies: A Canadian View on Military Professions in a Global Society." Unpublished paper in possession of author.

Oliver, Dean F. "Canadian Military Professional Development: The Way Ahead?" Paper presented at Conference of Defence Associations Institute XVth Annual Seminar, 1999 – The Profession of Arms in Canada: Past, Present and Future. Paper in possession of the author (Allan D. English).

Owens, Mackubin Thomas. "Military Ethos and 'Don't Ask, Don't Tell.'" *Providence Journal*, 31 December 1999. http://www.projo.com/report/pjb/stories/02989651.htm

Paret, Peter, ed. *Makers of Modern Strategy*. Princeton: Princeton Univ. Press, 1986.

Passey, Greg and David Crockett. "Psychological Consequences of Canadian UN Peacekeeping." Unpublished paper, Department of Psychiatry, University of British Columbia (revised 18 August 1997), Exhibit #51 Board of Inquiry – Croatia.

Paul, John and Jerome Lauglicht. *In Your Opinion: Leaders' and Voters' Attitudes on Defence and Disarmament*. Clarkson, ON: Canadian Peace Research Institute, 1963.

Pedersen, Jesper S. and Jesper S. Sorensen. *Organisational Cultures in Theory and Practice*. Aldershot: Avebury, 1989.

Peters, W.N. "Why is Strategy Difficult – In Canada?" Unpublished paper written for War Studies MA course, RMC. http: //wps.cfc.dnd.ca/irc/amsc/peters.html

Pheysey, Diana C. *Organizational Cultures: Types and Transformations*. London: Routledge, 1993.

Pinch, Franklin C. "Canada: Managing Change with Shrinking Resources." In Charles C. Moskos et al., eds. *The Postmodern Military: Armed Forces After the Cold War*, 156–81. New York: Oxford Univ. Press, 2000.

Preston, Adrian. "The Profession of Arms in Postwar Canada, 1945–1970." *World Politics* 23 (January 1971): 189–214.

Preston, Richard. "The Potential of the Military for Contributions to Conventional Deterrence in the 1970s." In R.B. Byers and Colin S. Gray, eds. *Canadian Military Professionalism: The Search for Identity*, 60–74. Toronto: Canadian Institute of International Affairs, 1973.

Reimer, Dennis J. "Dominant Maneuver and Precision Engagement." *Joint Forces Quarterly* (Winter 1996–97): 13–16.

Ricks, Thomas E. "On American Soil: The Widening Gap between the U.S. Military and U.S. Society." John M. Olin Institute for Strategic Studies Project on U.S. Post Cold-War Civil-Military Relations, Harvard Univ., May 1996. http://hdc-www.harvard.edu/cfia/olin/civmil.htm

Robbins, Stephen P. *Organizational Behaviour: Concepts, Controversies, Applications*. 5d. Englewood Cliffs, NJ: Prentice Hall, 1991.

Robbins, Stephen P. and Nancy Langton. *Organizational Behaviour: Concepts, Controversies, Applications.* Scarborough: Prentice Hall, 1999.

Rothenberg, Gunther. "Moltke, Schlieffen, and the Doctrine of Strategic Envelopment." In Peter Paret, ed. *Makers of Modern Strategy*, 296–325. Princeton: Princeton Univ. Press, 1986.

Sapolsky, Harvey M. "Interservice Competition: The Solution, Not the Problem." *Joint Force Quarterly* (Spring 1997): 50–3.

Sarkesian, Sam C., et al. *Soldiers, Society and National Security.* Boulder, CO: Lynne Rienner, 1995.

Schein, Edgar H. *Organizational Culture and Leadership*, 2d. San Francisco: Jossey-Bass, 1992.

Schermerhorn, John R. Jr., et al. *Organizational Behavior*, 6d. New York: John Wiley, 1997.

Schmitt, John F. "Command and (Out of) Control: The Military Implications of Complexity Theory." *Marine Corps Gazette* 82, no. 9 (September 1998): 55–8.

Semianiw, W. "Western Operational Theory: Breaking the Industrial Paradigm." Paper prepared for AMSC 1, 1998. (Available from Information Resource Centre, Canadian Forces College, Toronto.) http://bib.cfc.dnd.ca/webpacj/cfc.html

Shelley, C.R. "Crisis of Character? Ethical Development in the Canadian Officer Corps." *Canadian Defence Quarterly* 25, no. 4 (June 1996): 23–7.

Shy, John. "Jomini." In Peter Paret, ed. *Makers of Modern Strategy,* 143–85. Princeton: Princeton Univ. Press, 1986.

Skelton, William B. "Samuel P. Huntington and the Roots of the American Military Tradition." *The Journal of Military History* 60, no. 2 (April 1996): 325–9.

Sloan, Elinor C. *The Revolution in Military Affairs.* Montreal & Kingston: McGill-Queen's Univ. Press, 2002.

– "The United States and the Revolution in Military Affairs." Directorate of Strategic Analysis, DND, Ottawa, Project Report No. 9801, February 1998.

Smith, James M. "Air Force Culture and Cohesion." *Airpower Journal* 12, no. 3 (Fall 1998): 40–53.

Snider, Don M. "An Uninformed Debate on Military Culture." *Orbis* 43, no. 1 (Winter 1999): 15–26.

Soeters, J. and R. Recht. "Culture and Discipline in Military Academies: An International Comparison." *Journal of Political and Military Sociology* 26, no. 2 (Winter 1998): 169–89.

Spellman, Thomas Patrick. "The Role of Organizational Culture in the Leadership of United States Air Force Services Squadrons." Unpublished monograph, Cornell University, 1988. Copy in Information Resource Centre, Canadian Forces College, Toronto.

Stacey, C.P. *Arms, Men and Governments*, Ottawa: Queen's Printer, 1970.

Stanley, G.F.G. "Obedience to Whom? To What?" In Edgar Denton III, ed. *Limits of Loyalty,* 3–22. Waterloo, ON: Wilfrid Laurier Univ. Press, 1980.

Swain, Richard. "Filling the Void: The Operational Art and the US Army." In B.J.C. McKercher and Michael A. Hennessy, eds. *The Operational Art: Developments in the Theories of War,* 148–66. Westport, CT: Praeger, 1996.

Szafranski, Richard. "Annulling Marriages: Reframing the Roles, Missions, and Functions Debate." *Airpower Journal* 7, no. 4 (Winter 1993): 55–67.

– "Peer Competitors, the RMA (Revolution in Military Affairs), and New Concepts: Some Questions." *Naval War College Review* 49, no. 2 (Spring 1996): 113–19.

Terraine, John. *The Right of the Line.* London: Hodder and Stoughton, 1985.

Thériault, Gerry. "Democratic Civil-military Relations: A Canadian View." In Jim Hanson and Susan Nish, eds. *The Military in Modern Democratic Society,* 4–12. Toronto: Canadian Institute of Strategic Studies, November 1996.

Tse, David K., et al. "Cultural Differences in Conducting Intra- and Inter-Cultural Negotiations: A Sino-Canadian Comparison." *Journal of International Business Studies* 25, no. 3 (Third Quarter 1994): 537–49.

Ulmer, Walter F. Jr., et al. *American Military Culture in the Twenty-First Century.* Washington, DC: CSIS Press, 2000.

US Department of Defense, Joint Publication 0-2. *Unified Action Armed Forces* (February 1995). http//www.dtic.mil/doctrine/jel/new_pubs/primer.pdf

Van Creveld, Martin. "High Technology and the Transformation of War, Part 1." *RUSI Journal* 137, no. 5 (October 1992): 76–81.

– "High Technology and the Transformation of War, Part 2." *RUSI Journal* 137, no. 6 (December 1992): 61–4.

Van Riper, Paul K. and Robert H. Scales Jr. "Preparing for War in the 21st Century." *Parameters* 27 (Autumn 1997): 4–14.

Wakin, Malham M., ed. *War, Morality, and the Military Profession*, 2d. London: Westview Press, 1986.

Wallace, Bruce. "What Makes a Canadian?" *Maclean's* 112, no. 51 (20 December 1999): 32–6.

Walsh, Michael J. "Operations Other than War and Its Impact on Combat Training Readiness." Carlisle Barracks, PA: US Army War College, 1998.

Watson, William. *Globalization and the Meaning of Canadian Life.* Toronto: Univ. of Toronto Press, 1998.

Weigley, Russell F. "American Strategy from its Beginnings through the First World War." In Peter Paret, ed. *Makers of Modern Strategy*, 408–43. Princeton: Princeton Univ. Press, 1986.

– *The American Way of War.* Bloomington: Indiana Univ. Press, 1973.

Wild, W.R. "Army Culture." 1080–1–6004 (DLP3–4) NDHQ, Ottawa, July 1997. Unpublished paper. Copy in Information Resource Centre, Canadian Forces College, Toronto.

Winslow, Donna. "Misplaced Loyalties: The Role of Military Culture in the Breakdown of Discipline in Peace Operations." *Canadian Review of Sociology and Anthropology* 35, no. 3 (August 1998): 346–65.

Winter, Denis. *First of the Few.* Athens, GA: Univ. of Georgia Press, 1983.

Wise, S.F. *Canadian Airmen and the First World War.* Vol. 1 of *The Official History of the Royal Canadian Air Force*. Toronto: Univ. of Toronto Press, 1980.

Wood, Chris. "The Vanishing Border." *Maclean's*, 20 December 1999, 20–3.

Young, Richard J. "Clausewitz and His Influence on US and Canadian Military Doctrine." In Allan D. English, ed. *The Changing Face of War: Learning from History,* 9–21. Montreal & Kingston: McGill-Queen's Univ. Press, 1998.

Zoll, Donald A. "A Crisis in Self-Image: The Role of the Military in American Culture." *Parameters* 12, no. 4 (December 1982): 24–31.

Index